Isaiah 60   26/10/10

Liz
28/10/10

The
Better Covenant

The
Better
Covenant

WATCHMAN NEE

Christian Fellowship Publishers, Inc.
New York

ISBN 0–935008–55–1

Available from the Publishers at:

11515 Allecingie Parkway
Richmond, Virginia 23235

Printed in the United States of America

PREFACE

The New Covenant is full of God's grace. In order to enjoy such grace each one who belongs to the Lord must know what this New Covenant is. How sad that many of the Lord's people today neither appreciate nor understand this New Covenant. For this reason we have a burden to release some messages on the New Covenant. Even so, the New Covenant is such a comprehensive subject that we cannot exhaust its richness with our limited learning, experience and words. Still, we look to God's grace and are willing to share with His children the little we have received. Our earnest prayer is that God would enable us to know something of the New Covenant and lead us into its spiritual reality.

The Editor
Gospel Book Room
Shanghai, China

November 1953

CONTENTS

At a conference held in Shanghai, China, in 1932, the author gave a series of messages on the New Covenant. These were later edited and published in Chinese in 1953 by the Gospel Book Room, Shanghai. They are now being translated into English for the first time.

Scripture quotations are from the American Standard Version of the Bible (1901), unless otherwise indicated.

Introduction

For this is my blood of the covenant, which is poured out for many unto remission of sins. (Matt. 26.28; many ancient authorities insert *new* before "covenant")

For finding fault with them, he saith, Behold, the days come, saith the Lord, that I will make a new covenant with the house of Israel and with the house of Judah; not according to the covenant that I made with their fathers in the day that I took them by the hand to lead them forth out of the land of Egypt; for they continued not in my covenant, and I regarded them not, saith the Lord. For this is the covenant that I will make with the house of Israel after those days, saith the Lord; I will put my laws into their mind, and on their heart also will I write them: and I will be to them a God, and they shall be to me a people: and they shall not teach every man his fellow-citizen, and every man his brother, saying, Know the Lord: for all shall know me, from the least to the greatest of them. For I will be merciful to their iniquities, and their sins will I remember no more. In that he saith, A new covenant, he hath made the first old. But that which is becoming old and waxeth aged is nigh unto vanishing away. (Heb. 8.8-13)

This is the covenant that I will make with them after those days, saith the Lord: I will put my laws on their heart, and upon their mind also will I write them. (Heb. 10.16)

Behold, the days come, saith Jehovah, that I will make a

new covenant with the house of Israel, and with the house of
Judah: not according to the covenant that I made with their
fathers in the day that I took them by the hand to bring them
out of the land of Egypt; which my covenant they brake, although I was a husband unto them, saith Jehovah. But this is
the covenant that I will make with the house of Israel after
those days, saith Jehovah: I will put my law in their inward
parts, and in their heart will I write it; and I will be their
God, and they shall be my people. And they shall teach no
more every man his neighbor, and every man his brother,
saying, Know Jehovah; for they shall all know me, from the
least of them unto the greatest of them, saith Jehovah: for I
will forgive their iniquity, and their sin will I remember no
more. (Jer. 31.31–34)

Who also made us sufficient as ministers of a new covenant; not of the letter, but of the spirit: for the letter killeth,
but the spirit giveth life. (2 Cor. 3.6)

Now the God of peace, who brought again from the dead
the great shepherd of the sheep with the blood of an eternal
covenant, even our Lord Jesus, make you perfect in every
good thing to do his will, working in us that which is well-
pleasing in his sight, through Jesus Christ, to whom be the
glory for ever and ever. Amen. (Heb. 13.20–21)

One

The New Covenant is the foundation of all spiritual life. It
is due to the New Covenant that our sin may be forgiven and
our conscience may regain its peace. It is because of the New
Covenant that we are able to obey God and to do the things
well-pleasing to Him. It is also through the New Covenant that
we can commune with God directly and know Him deeply
within. Were it not for the New Covenant we would have no
assurance of forgiveness, no power to obey and to do God's will,

and no inward fellowship with God and deep knowledge of Him. Thank God, there is a New Covenant. He has covenanted with us, therefore we can rest on His covenant.

> *Resting on the faithfulness of Christ our Lord,*
> *Resting on the fulness of His own sure word,*
> *Resting on His wisdom, on His love and pow'r,*
> *Resting on his covenant from hour to hour.*
> —FRANCES RIDLEY HAVERGAL

This hymn-writer understood what the New Covenant is, and so he rested on the covenant of the Lord.

Two

The eternal purpose of God is revealed in the New Covenant. He who is the Lord's must know this covenant, else he shall not be able to apprehend God's eternal purpose in his experience. We are told that "death reigned from Adam until Moses, . . . sin reigned in death . . ." (Rom. 5.14, 21). Now during this period the eternal purpose of God was not yet revealed. But when God "preached the gospel beforehand unto Abraham, saying, In thee shall all the nations be blessed" (Gal. 3.8), something of the shadow of grace was shown to us, yet the substance of grace was still unseen. "The law was given through Moses" (John 1.17), yet "the law came in besides" (Rom. 5.20). It is never included in the eternal purpose of God. "All the prophets and the law prophesied until John" (Matt. 11.13), but "grace and truth came through Jesus Christ" (John 1.17). Therefore, with Christ comes the dispensation of grace, the New Covenant, and the revelation of the eternal purpose of God. God's eternal purpose is revealed in the New Covenant. By knowing the latter we may expect the former to be accomplished in our lives. Otherwise, we will only be able to touch the fringe, not the substance, of salvation. If we know somewhat concerning the New Covenant, it can then be said that we have touched the greatest treasure in the universe!

What is the eternal purpose of God? To state it simply, it is God working himself into the man whom He has created. God takes pleasure in joining himself with man that the latter may have His life and nature. In eternity, before time began and before heaven and earth and man were created, God had already conceived this purpose. He desired that man should be like Him, glorified and conformed to the image of His Son (Eph. 1.4, 5; Rom. 8.29, 30). For this reason, He created man in His own image (Gen. 1.27). He then put the man He created in the garden of Eden, wherein were the tree of life and the tree of the knowledge of good and evil. God only forbade man to eat the fruit of the tree of the knowledge of good and evil. In other words, God was indicating to man how he should eat the fruit of the tree of life, though the man himself must choose actively. According to the revelation of the Bible, the tree of life points to God (Ps. 36.9; John 1.4, 11.25, 14.6; 1 John 5.12). If man were to eat the fruit of the tree of life he would have life, and God would enter into him.

We know how the first Adam—the first man God created— failed. Instead of receiving God's life, Adam took the fruit of the tree of the knowledge of good and evil and was thereby alienated from the lifegiving God. Nevertheless, we praise and thank God, for though the first man was defeated and fell, the Second Man—that is, the last Adam (1 Cor. 15.45, 47)—has arrived at the eternal purpose of God. In the whole universe there is at least one man who is commingled with God: Jesus of Nazareth, who is at once God and man, man and God. The Lord Jesus is "the Word [that] became flesh, and dwelt among us . . ., full of grace and truth" (John 1.14). Though "no man hath seen God at any time; the only begotten Son, who is in the bosom of the Father, he hath declared him" (John 1.18). God's eternal purpose is to so work himself into man as to conform him into the image of His Son. This is the New Covenant.

Three

What do we mean by saying today is the dispensation of the New Covenant? We will mention it only briefly now and explain it in more detail in the third chapter. We know God has never made any covenant with the Gentiles: we who are Gentiles did not have the Old Covenant; how then can we have the New? Hebrews 8.8 plainly informs us that one day God will make a new covenant with the house of Israel and the house of Judah. Strictly speaking, the New Covenant will come only after those days (Heb. 8.10), that is, it will ultimately be established only at the commencement of the millennium. This being the case, how can we say that *today* is the dispensation of the New Covenant? This is due to no other reason than that the Lord treats His church in accordance with the principle of the New Covenant. He places the church under the New Covenant principle for the church to communicate and deal with Him according to this covenant until He accomplishes all that He desires. "This is my blood of the [new] covenant," says the Lord (Matt. 26.28 mg.). He inaugurates the New Covenant with His blood that we might foretaste its blessings. For us to say that today is the dispensation of the New Covenant is an evidence of the special grace of the Lord. We must therefore know experientially what the New Covenant is so that we may live in this new dispensation.

Four

In order to know the New Covenant we need to first understand what a covenant is; and to understand a covenant we must know what God's promise and God's fact are. We shall therefore speak a little about God's promise and God's fact before we move on to the subject of God's covenant — the New Covenant and its characteristics. We shall deal particularly with the following important matters: how the law is put within man and inscribed upon his heart; how the power of life operates; how God becomes our God in the law of life and how we become God's people in this law of life; and lastly, how we actually know inwardly so that we may have deeper knowledge of God.

1 | God's Promise and God's Fact

In the word of God some writers speak of the responsibilities which God requires men to bear, while some speak of the grace which God desires to give to men. In other words, some refer to God's demand while some refer to God's grace. Many commandments, teachings, statutes, and so forth are expressive of God's demand on men; that is, that for which God requires men to be responsible. But every spiritual blessing in the heavenly places in Christ (Eph. 1.3)—such as an inheritance incorruptible and undefiled and unfading (1 Peter 1.4)—is indicative of the grace which God is pleased to accomplish and give to us. So far as the word of God goes, grace may be classified according to three categories: (1) the promise God gives to us, (2) the fact God has already accomplished for us, and (3) the covenant God makes with man, showing what He is determined to do. As God's promise and God's fact are different, so God's covenant is different from God's promise and God's fact. God's covenant, however, includes His promise and His fact. It may be outlined as follows:

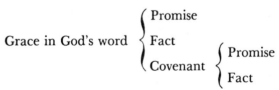

Let us first look at what God's promise is.

GOD'S PROMISE

Promise is different from fact. Promise points to the future, whereas fact refers to the past. Promise shows what will be done, but fact reveals what is done already. Promise tells of what God will do for man; fact tells what God has already accomplished for man. Promise indicates what God will do in response to man's doing; fact attests to what God has accomplished for us because He loves us and knows our inability. There are many promises with conditions; that is to say, if we fulfill certain conditions we shall receive what is promised. Fact, though, does not demand our begging or imploring; it only requires us to see and to believe.

Let us offer some illustrations to explain the difference between promise and fact.

The Lord Jesus comforted His disciples, saying, "Let not your heart be troubled: believe in God, believe also in me . . .; for I go to prepare a place for you. And . . . I come again, and will receive you unto myself" (John 14.1-3). This is a promise which will become a fact on the day of the Lord's return.

He also said this to the disciples: "It is expedient for you that I go away; for if I go not away, the Comforter will not come unto you; but if I go, I will send him unto you" (John 16.7). This too is a promise which is turned into a fact on the day of the Lord's resurrection when He "breathed on them, and saith unto them, Receive ye the Holy Spirit" (see John 20.19-22).

Again He told the disciples, "Behold, I send forth the promise of my Father upon you: but tarry ye in the city, until ye be clothed with power from on high" (Luke 24.49). This is the promise of promises, which too becomes a fact on the day of Pentecost when the Holy Spirit came upon them (see Acts 2.1-4). But this promise is conditional in that the disciples must wait in the city.

We may also use a parable to analyze the difference between promise and fact. Suppose A and B are friends. A is sick in bed, having no strength to work nor money to buy the necessities of life. B loves A, so he says to A, "Tomorrow morning I will work for you and bring you the money for purchasing your necessities." This is B's promise to A. Sure enough, B goes forth the next morning and works for A and subsequently brings him the money he needs to buy necessities. This shows that B's promise to A has now become a fact. If A believes in B's promise, counting B's word as trustworthy, he will have hope and rest on the first day, although he comes into actual enjoyment on the second day.

Several Principles Regarding God's Promise

The Bible shows us several principles regarding God's promise, such as the following:

(1) "Honor thy father and mother (which is the first commandment with promise), that it may be well with thee, and thou mayest live long on the earth" (Eph. 6.2-3). This promise is conditional. Not every person is blessed and lives long on the earth; only the one who honors his father and mother may be well and live long on the earth. If one does not fullfill the condition herein prescribed, he will not receive the promised blessing nor the promised longevity.

(2) "Now, O Jehovah God, let thy promise unto David my father be established" (2 Chron. 1.9). This indicates how prayer or *asking* is needed for the realization of promise (see also 1 Kings 8.56).

(3) "After the number of the days in which ye spied out the land, even forty days, for every day a year, shall ye bear your iniquities, even forty years, and ye shall know my alienation ['the revoking of my promise'—ASV mg.]" (Num. 14.34). This reveals how a promise may be *revoked* if men are unfaithful to

God's promise and fail to fulfill its condition. Of the Israelites who came out of Egypt, only two persons — Caleb and Joshua — were able to enter Canaan; the rest fell dead in the wilderness (see Num. 26.65). Clearly God abrogated His promise towards the unfaithful people. (Though Jacob and Joseph died in Egypt, they were nonetheless buried in Canaan. Because they were faithful to God to the end, therefore God did not revoke His promise to them. See Gen. 46.3-4, 49.29-32, 50.12-13 and 24-25; Joshua 24.32).

(4) "For not through the law was the promise to Abraham or to his seed that he should be heir of the world, but through the righteousness of faith. For if they that are of the law are heirs, faith is made void, and the promise is made of none effect" (Rom. 4.13-14). This implies that if aside from God man uses the strength of flesh and blood, or adds anything to it, the promise may become void.

(5) "And these all, having had witness borne to them through their faith, received not the promise, God having provided some better thing concerning us, that apart from us they should not be made perfect" (Heb. 11.39-40). Also, "Ye have need of patience, that, having done the will of God, ye may receive the promise" (Heb. 10.36). This suggests that *patience* must be exercised for receiving God's promise at the right time.

By the above passages of the Scriptures we may perceive the following four principles regarding God's promise:

(1) God's promise needs our asking Him to fullfill it.

(2) If God's promise is conditional, it will be given only upon its condition being fullfilled; otherwise it may be revoked.

(3) If man in his natural strength does anything to the promise, or if he adds something to it, the promise may also be declared void.

(4) God's promise is to be realized at God's time.

How God's Promise Is Realized in Us

Each time we notice a promise in the word of God, we ought to pray fervently till the Spirit of God rises within us and makes us feel that this promise is meant for us. If it is unconditional we should immediately exercise faith to receive it, trusting that God will do what He has promised to us and commencing to praise and thank Him. But if this promise is conditional, we need first to fulfill the requirement and then pray that God perform according to His faithfulness and righteousness. Pray till faith springs up from within; then cease praying and begin praising God. It shall not be long before we see God's promise being realized.

Let us illustrate this with some real experiences. (1) At a certain place there were a few sisters who usually asked God at the beginning of each year for a promise as to their annual support. One sister, sensing her own weakness, told the Lord of her need. The word which the Lord gave her was: "Christ . . . to you-ward is not weak, but is powerful in you" (2 Cor. 13.3). Having received such a word, she was immediately strengthened. Another sister was of the anxious type. She became frightened whenever she thought of the past and looked forward to the future. She too told the Lord of her actual condition. Consequently she received a promise from the Lord, saying, "Fear thou not, for I am with thee; be not dismayed, for I am thy God; I will strengthen thee; yea, I will help thee; yea, I will uphold thee with the right hand of my righteousness" (Is. 41.10). The six I's and my's and the three will's in this passage caused her to bow her head and worship God. She was moved to tears of joy and touched by the fullness of promises. Thereafter, whenever she was faced with difficulty or temptation she would read this word to herself as well as to God. Thus was she strengthened, helped and sustained through many years. These sisters had among them many similar experiences. The promises which God gave suited perfectly their needs.

They earnestly sought God for promises, and at the end of each year when they counted the Lord's grace they could prove how often God's promises had comforted and supported them through the year.

(2) A child of God asked Him for a promise concerning her livelihood. One day she read these words: "Be ye free from the love of money; content with such things as ye have: for himself hath said, I will in no wise fail thee, neither will I in any wise forsake thee" (Heb. 13.5). She was both surprised and gladdened by this word. Such promise is conditional: one must first be free from the greed of gain and be content with what he already has, before he can experience the Lord's abiding support and supply. She said amen and amen to this promise. In her past twenty years she on the one hand maintained the principle that "if any will not work, neither let him eat" (2 Thess. 3.10) and on the other hand experienced the Lord's causing neither a handful of meal in the jar to waste nor a little oil in the cruse to fail (see 1 Kings 17.8-16). The Lord had not failed her nor forsaken her.

(3) A child of God was sick for a long time. Just at the point of utter despair, she remembered the word in Romans 8.13: "If ye live after the flesh, ye must die; but if by the Spirit ye put to death the deeds of the body, ye shall live." It was a turning point in her life. She began to deal with everything in accordance with the light the Lord had given her. Even so, there was still no improvement in her health. She therefore prayed one day as follows: "Lord, if the word of Romans 8.13 is given to me, then give me another promise." She confessed how unworthy she was and acknowledged how little faith she had. At that very moment there came a word like this within her: "God is not a man that he should lie." She was not aware that such a word existed in the Bible. As she consulted a concordance she found it was indeed recorded in Numbers 23.19, "God is not a man, that he should lie, neither the son of man, that he should repent: Hath he said, and will he not do it? Or hath he spoken,

and will he not make it good?" Her heart was therefore full of joy and her mouth full of praise. Eventually God took away her disease.

(4) At a certain stage in their spiritual pilgrimage several children of God entered upon a situation not unlike that which is described in Psalm 66—"Thou broughtest us into the net; thou layedst a sore burden upon our loins. Thou didst cause men to ride over our heads" (vv.11, 12a). Nevertheless, God also gave them the following promise: "We went through fire and through water; but thou broughtest us out into a wealthy place" (v.12b). This promise strengthened as well as comforted them.

(5) Several of God's children were in great trial. Each time they prayed they were comforted and strengthened by this promise—"There hath no temptation taken you but such as man can bear: but God is faithful, who will not suffer you to be tempted above that ye are able; but will with the temptation make also the way of escape, that ye may be able to endure it" (1 Cor. 10.13).

(6) A servant of the Lord met severe trial. It looked as though a high mountain were standing in his way. He climbed until totally exhausted and deeply despondent, until there was left in him but a tiny speck of hope—a hope reflected in these words: "even unto this present hour"; "even until now" (1 Cor. 4.11-13). This was enough, however, to carry this servant of the Lord over the mountain. "Even until now" was he looked upon as the filth of the world and the offscouring of all things; nevertheless, "even until now" he was able to stand. How trying to man is time: even so, God's promise enables him to stand the testing of time and to stand "even until now."

(7) Several disciples were distressed by the waves and cried out to the Lord. "Be of good cheer," said the Lord; "it is I; be not afraid" (Matt. 14.24-27). When this promise came their troubled hearts were stilled, and the waves lost their force by which to send them to the bottom of the sea.

GOD'S FACT

Even though we cannot find the word "fact" in the Bible, we do discover many accomplished facts in the word of God. In other words, fact refers to the finished work of God.

God made the promise in the Old Testament period that the Lord Jesus would be born of a virgin (see Is. 7.14); so "when the fulness of the time came, God sent forth his Son, born of a woman, born under the law, that he might redeem them that were under the law, that we might receive the adoption of sons" (Gal. 4.4,5). The promise in Isaiah that "a virgin shall conceive, and bear a son" is now already fulfilled. It has become an accomplished fact. So too is the crucifixion of the Lord Jesus a fact accomplished. For He offered himself once and has obtained eternal redemption for us (see Heb. 9.12). Since this is fact, no one can now ask the Lord to come and die for his redemption. Equally factual is the coming of the Holy Spirit, for this is forever accomplished. Being a fact, there is absolutely no room for our praying that the Holy Spirit come, nor is there any need for such prayer. (Of course, this observation is directed to the *fact* of the Holy Spirit's coming, not to the personal experience of the Holy Spirit coming upon us).

Besides these facts God has achieved much more in Christ. The Bible tells us that all things which pertain to life and godliness have been achieved in Christ. For instance, in Ephesians 1.3 it is said: "God . . . hath blessed us with every spiritual blessing in the heavenly places in Christ." Verse 4 immediately follows by saying "even as . . .", and this continues on in one long breath until the end of verse 14 is reached; thus indicating that all these verses allude to the spiritual blessings in the heavenly places. These all serve to explain what Peter means when he declares "that his divine power hath granted unto us all things that pertain unto life and godliness" (2 Peter 1.3). They are all in Christ as accomplished facts.

As regards God's promise there is the possibility of it going unrealized—or even being abolished—if we do not ask or do not fulfill the condition therein. But God's fact will not fail to be actualized in us for our lack of asking. Since it is already a fact, it needs no asking. (Again, this points to God's fact itself, no to our individual experience of it). Never once does God require us to do anything special in order to obtain His fact. We need only believe in it, and we shall have it. God's promise can be delayed, but God's fact is never detained. It is altogether impossible for us to accept God's fact and to wait for several years before He gives it to us. Whatever God has already accomplished and given us in Christ cannot be postponed to the future. For if God should hesitate in giving to us, it would be contradictory to fact. We can illustrate this point with two cases.

Case 1

Ephesians 2.5-6 tells us of the great love with which God has loved us: "Even when we were dead through our trespasses, [God] made us alive together with Christ (by grace have ye been saved), and raised us up with him, and made us to sit with him in the heavenly places, in Christ Jesus." Is what is said here God's promise or God's fact? The Scriptures show us that all these things are facts. It is God who has made us alive together with Christ, raised us up together with Christ, and seated us together with Christ in the heavenly places. These are all accomplished facts. Being accomplished facts, we need to thank and praise God and to have manifested to Satan that we have indeed been raised and ascended with Christ. This is not by our assuming a certain attitude in order to *be* raised and ascended, but our taking the position of having *been* raised and ascended with Christ.

Let us be clear that the life which all who belong to the Lord have received is none other than the risen and ascended life. If any surmise that this life is not given unless it is first asked for, he doubtless does not know God's accomplished fact. As a matter of truth, God has already granted us all things pertaining to life and godliness. We need not ask, we need only take. Hallelujah! Praise the Lord for the glorious fact, the accomplished fact, the fact accomplished by Christ and given to us by God.

Case 2

Romans 6.6 reads: "Knowing this, that our old man was crucified with him, that the body of sin might be done away, that so we should no longer be in bondage to sin." This verse mentions three things: sin, the old man, and the body of sin. The sin here points to that sinful nature which reigns in man (Rom. 6.14, 7.17). The old man speaks of the self which delights in listening to sin. And the body of sin means this body of ours which is sin's puppet and which actually sins. Thus sin reigns within as master. It directs the old man to cause the body to sin. The old man represents all which comes from Adam; the old man naturally inclines toward sin. He it is who steers the body to sin. In order for us not to sin, some have suggested that the root of sin needs to be eradicated from within; whereas others have expressed the thought that we must harshly suppress the outside body. Yet God's way is totally different from man's. He neither eradicates the root of sin nor ill-treats the body; instead, He deals with the old man.

"Our old man *was* crucified with him." As the Lord Jesus has already been crucified, so our old man too has been crucified. This is a fact, that which God has accomplished through Christ.

"The body of sin might be done away" can more accurately be translated, according to the original, as: "the body of sin might be unemployed." Since God has already crucified our old man with Christ on the cross, this body of sin is accordingly unemployed. Although our sinful nature still exists and is yet actively tempting us, the old man who was formerly used by sin has been crucified with Christ on the cross. So that sin can no longer reign over us, and we are freed from it.

Nevertheless, as people look at themselves—noticing how undone and prone to sin they are—they most likely will ask God for second grace or for some renewed work, such as the eradication of the root of sin, so as to be delivered from sin. Or they will concede that even though Christ was crucified their old man was not crucified; and therefore they ask God to crucify their old man. But the more they ask Him to crucify their old man, the more active and oppressive he seems to become.

Why is this so? This is because they only know God's promise without knowing God's fact, or in taking God's fact as God's promise, they use the wrong way of approach. God has quite definitely declared that their old man *was* crucified with Christ, yet they misconstrue it to mean that God *promises* to crucify their old man. Hence they ask God to do it. Whenever they sin, they consider their old man as still uncrucified, and so they once again ask God to crucify their old man. Every time they are tempted to sin, they reckon their old man as not yet having been thoroughly dealt with; consequently, they feel they must petition God again to deal with their old man. They are ignorant that their old man being crucified with Christ is an accomplished fact. How different is this from a promise. In spite of their persistent praying, they will make no gain. All they can do is cry out: "Wretched man that I am!"

We ought to know that Romans 6.6 is a basic experience for each one who belongs to the Lord. It is imperative for us to ask the Spirit of the Lord for revelation that we may see how our old man *was* crucified with Christ. Thus shall we be able to believe according to God's word that we have indeed died to sin (Rom. 6. 10-11). No matter how temptation may sometimes come—causing us to feel as though our old man has not died—we will nonetheless believe in what God has done rather than in our feeling and experience. When we truly see this as a fact we shall find that the experience of it will naturally follow. Let us notice that God's fact does not become factual because we so believe; instead, we believe so because God's fact is already factual.

What is belief? God has said that our old man was crucified with Christ, so we say that our old man *was* crucified with Christ. That our old man is dead is a fact. It is a fact accomplished by God through Christ; and God can do no more. And neither can we do anything except believe in the truthfulness of God's word. Our need towards God's fact is not praying that God will do it, but believing that He has already done it. As soon as we believe in God's fact, we shall have the experience of it. God's appointed order is fact, faith and experience. This is a great principle in spiritual life which should be remembered.

Some Principles Regarding God's Fact

From the cases which have just been presented, we may derive certain principles regarding God's fact:

(1) Find out, first of all, what *is* God's fact. This requires the revelation of the Holy Spirit.

(2) Then, in knowing a certain thing to be indeed God's fact, one should lay hold of God's word and believe that he has already become whatever God's word has pronounced, trusting that he is what God's fact is.

(3) Through such faith as this, one should on the one hand thank God for what he already is, and on the other hand act upon it—thus showing forth what he really is.

(4) Whenever he is tempted or tested, the person must believe that God's word and God's fact are more dependable than his own feeling. If he fully believes in God's word, God will be responsible for giving him the experience. Should a person turn to his own past negative experience he will be defeated and will not have any future positive experience. To believe in

God's fact is *our* responsibility; to give us the proper experience is *His* responsibility. By our believing in God's fact, our spiritual life will daily advance.

(5) Fact requires faith from man, for faith is the only way to substantiate fact and translate it into experience. God's fact is in Christ. A man must be in Christ before he can enjoy God's fact in Christ. We must be united with Christ, then shall we experience the accomplished fact of God in Christ. Let us keep well in mind that at the time we were saved we were united with Christ, for we are already in Christ (see 1 Cor. 1.30, Gal. 3.27, Rom. 6.3). Only, that many who are "in Christ" do not "abide" in Him. They do not stand by faith on the position which God has given them in Christ, thus lacking the effectiveness of God's fact in their lives. We must therefore *abide* in Christ as well as *be* in Christ if God's fact is to become our experience.

Need to See

We have repeatedly declared that God's fact is what He has already done; we ought not ask Him to do anything more. But if we do not see the genuineness of God's fact, then we should ask God to grant us revelation and light that we may see. It is by the spirit of wisdom and revelation that we may truly know (Eph. 1.17-18). This is something for which we may ask. We ask for *seeing*. We do not ask God to *do* this thing, but we do ask Him to make us see what He has already *done*. May this distinction be very clear to us. And to help us, we will use some substantial illustrations to explain it.

ILLUSTRATION A

A sister, before she saw the fact of her being "in Christ," thought she must strive through her own effort to get into Christ; yet she did not know how to get in. One day she heard this word: "Of [God] are ye in Christ Jesus" (1 Cor. 1.30). Inwardly she saw that God had already put her in Christ, so she had no need to get in.

ILLUSTRATION B

Before they could say that "our old man was crucified with [Christ]," a few of God's children were either trying hard to crucify their old man or asking God to crucify their old man. The result was predictable. How can anyone crucify his old man? The more they tried to crucify the old man, the more active he became. The more they petitioned God to do it, the more confused they grew. Until one day God opened their eyes to see that He had already crucified their old man with Christ, and then they realized how foolish were their past efforts and prayers.

ILLUSTRATION C

One sister was never clear concerning the fact of the outpouring of the Holy Spirit. On a certain evening she shut herself in her room and read Acts 2. She asked God to give her revelation as she read. God opened her eyes to see three points in this chapter:

(1) Christ has been exalted to the right hand of God and has received from the Father the promise of the Holy Spirit whom Christ has poured forth (v.33).

(2) God has made Him both Lord and Christ (v.36).

(3) This promise (of the Holy Spirit whom Christ has received and poured forth) is given to the Israelites and their children and to all that are afar off (v.39).

She saw that the outpouring of the Holy Spirit is a fact. Having repented and been baptized in the name of Jesus Christ, she was included among those that were afar off. She therefore had a share in the promise of the Holy Spirit. Seeing this, she was full of joy and praised the Lord incessantly.

May we reiterate that concerning God's fact we need not petition Him to do it; all we need to ask for is that we may see He has already done it. We do not ask Him to put us now in Christ; we only ask Him to show us that He has already put us in Christ. Similarly, we ask not that God will now crucify our old man; we ask, instead, that He cause us to see He has already crucified our old man with Christ. In like manner, we do not ask God to pour forth from heaven the Holy Spirit now; rather, we ask that we may see that the Holy Spirit has already been poured. (Acts 1.13-14 says that the apostles with the women and Mary the mother of Jesus, together with His brethren, continued steadfastly in prayer with one accord. 2.1 indicates that the day of Pentecost was now come, and the disciples were gathered in one place, for the Holy Spirit had not yet been poured forth. 8.15-17, however, tells us that Peter and John prayed for the believers in Samaria and laid hands on them that they might receive the Holy Spirit. The apostles did not pray for the outpouring of the Holy Spirit from heaven. Such outpouring from heaven is a fact, while the coming of the Holy Spirit upon a person is an experience.) What we need to do is to ask God to show us the reality of His fact. And as soon as we see this inwardly we will naturally believe and thus experience it.

Let us now sum up the basic differences between God's promise and God's fact. In the Bible a promise indicates the word which God has spoken before He does the thing, while a fact proves to be God's word after He has done it. As to God's promise, we need to accept it by faith; but as to God's fact, we must not only accept it by faith but also begin to enjoy it as fact accomplished. It is consequently of great importance that we distinguish God's fact and God's promise while reading His word. Whenever we read of the grace of God—that is, of what God has wrought for us—we should ask the question: Is this a promise or is this a fact? If it is a promise and is conditional, we must first fulfill the condition and then pray until God gives us an inner assurance that this promise is for us. Thus shall we have faith that He has heard us, and we shall most naturally begin to praise Him. Although what God has promised is yet to be realized, we have the faith to accept it as though it were already in our hand. But if the matter turns out to be a fact, we should immediately exercise faith to thank Him, saying, "O God, this is indeed already so." We believe we are really so, and we act as if we are so. Thus shall we prove our faith.

Here are just a few more reminders:

(1) Before we seek the promise of the Lord we must first deal with impure faith, since a person with a confused mind or heated emotion may easily take this or that as God's promise to him. He seems to get a promise for today as well as for yesterday. He chooses them as in a lottery; and these promises come in quite handy. Yet such so-called promises of God are, in nine out of ten cases, untrustworthy and deceptive. (This is not to imply that God's promises are undependable; it simply means that these are what the person deems to be God's promises, being in reality only his own wishful thinking rather than God-given promises). Moreover, a prejudiced, strong-willed, or subjective person tends to grasp as God's promise that in God's word which is retained in his mind, which is suited to his desire, or which is subjectively interpreted. This is often undependable, and so will cause much disappointment, and even doubt concerning God's word. For this reason, before we seek God's promise we must ask Him to enlighten our heart that we may know ourselves. We need to ask Him to cleanse our heart and give us grace so that we may be willing to give up ourselves and wait quietly upon God. Then shall His promise impress itself spontaneously and clearly upon the deepest recess of our heart.

(2) Having received God's promise, we should begin to use it. Charles Spurgeon once said: Believers, I beg you not to treat the promises of the Lord as antiques in an exhibition. You should rather daily use them as springs of consolation, and trust the Lord always in times of trial. Such words by Spurgeon were doubtlessly spoken out of much experience.

(3) He who really has God's promise is usually restful and calm in his demeanor, for to him that promise is as good as realized. When Paul was constrained by the Lord while in Corinth, he was given a vision, in which the Lord said to him: "Be not afraid, but speak and hold not thy peace: for I am with thee, and no man shall set on thee to harm thee." So he stayed there a year and six months. (Acts 18.9-11) Again, when he met with danger from the sea on his journey to Rome, he could stand among his fellow passengers and declare: "Sirs, be of good cheer: for I believe God, that it shall be even so as it hath been spoken unto me." He not only believed God's promise but also used God's promise to promise and comfort others. Let us further observe that "when he had said this, and had taken bread, he gave thanks to God in the presence of all; and he brake it, and began to eat." Such was Paul's attitude towards the promise of God. This created such a deep impression on his fellow passengers that they were "all of good cheer, and themselves also took food" (Acts 27.23-25, 35-36).

A saint once said that each and every promise of God is built upon four foundations; namely, God's righteousness, God's holiness, God's grace, and God's truth. God's righteousness keeps Him from being unfaithful; God's holiness keeps him from being deceitful; God's grace, from being forgetful; and God's truth, from being changeful. And another saint of God proclaimed this: that a promise though tarried will not tarry long. And the psalmist too declares to his Lord: "Remember the word unto thy servant, because thou has made me to hope" (Ps. 119.49). This is a most powerful prayer. The promise of God gives us living hope. Hallelujah!

(4) After we once have seen God's fact, faith keeps looking at that fact, reckoning it as factual. Whenever we experience failure we should find out its cause and condemn its deed. In case we doubt—even denying God's fact on account of our failure—it proves we have an evil heart of unbelief (see Heb. 3.12). We must ask God to take it away.

Let us see that "we are become partakers of Christ, if we hold fast the beginning of our confidence firm unto the end" (Heb. 3.14).

2 | God's Covenant

Three things are included in God's gracious word—God's promise, God's fact, and God's covenant. In the first chapter we touched upon God's promise and God's fact; we shall now proceed to discuss God's covenant. All those whose hearts have been taught by grace will praise Him, saying, How very great and precious is it that God makes covenant with man!

God's promise is truly invaluable. In times of sickness, pain and trouble His promise is to us "as streams of water in a dry place, as the shade of a great rock in a weary land" (Is. 32.2).

Yet God's fact is easier for us to possess than God's promise. For He gives us not only the promise which is soon to be fulfilled but also the fact which is already accomplished. Truly He has put the treasure in earthen vessels "that the exceeding greatness of the power may be of God, and not from ourselves" (2 Cor. 4.7).

But today God not only grants us His promise and the fact which is already accomplished in Christ but He also covenants with us as well. His covenant is even more glorious than His promise and His fact. In making covenant with man God condescends himself to be bound and restricted by an agreement. He is willing to forfeit His liberty in the covenant in order to facilitate our possessing what He wants us to possess. The Most High God, the Creator of the heavens and the earth, stoops to make covenant with man. Such grace is beyond comparison. We can only bow and worship before the God of grace.

THE MEANING OF COVENANT

What does a covenant mean? A covenant speaks of faithfulness and of legality. It is not primarily concerned with pleasure and grace. A covenant is to be executed according to faithfulness, justice and law. If we make a covenant with people, stipulating in it all the things that we will do, we will be breaking our word and be faithless in case we do not perform according to this agreement. We will be looked upon as unrighteous and dishonest. We will have instantly lowered our moral standard; and furthermore, we will be judged by law as violators of covenant.

From this we can readily see that when God makes covenant with man He places himself in a circumscribed position. Originally He could treat us according to His own pleasure. He could deal with us in grace or without grace. He could either save us or not save us. Before He makes a covenant, God has the sovereign right to do whatever He likes. But after He has made it He must act in accordance with the written words of the covenant, for He is bound by it.

So far as the covenant itself is concerned, it now becomes a matter of faithfulness, not a matter of grace. Viewing it from the standpoint of God's willingness to bind himself in covenant with man, it is without doubt the highest expression of God's grace. How He has condescended to stand on the same level with man and thus place himself in a covenant! And once God has made a covenant He thereafter is under its restriction. Whether He likes it or not, God cannot violate His own covenant. Oh, how great and how noble is the fact of God making covenant with man!

WHY GOD MAKES COVENANT WITH MAN

Why should God make covenant with man? To understand

this question, we must trace back to the first time when God made such an arrangement with man. Strictly speaking, the first instance in the Old Testament of God making covenant with man occurred during the days of Noah. Before his time God had not made any covenant with man. Hence the covenant God made with Noah can be considered the earliest.

God Expresses His Mind in Covenant

From the instance of God making covenant with Noah, we are to understand how very difficult it is for God to make men know His mind. During the days of Noah mankind sinned so terribly that their iniquity could be spoken of as being full; consequently, God destroyed them with a flood. Yet He was mindful not only of Noah and his family but also of many living creatures. He wanted to preserve their lives. So He made a covenant with Noah, saying,

> I will establish my covenant with thee; and thou shalt come into the ark, thou, and thy sons, and thy wife, and thy sons' wives with thee. And of every living thing of all flesh, two of every sort shalt thou bring into the ark, to keep them alive with thee; they shall be male and female. Of the birds after their kind, and of the cattle after their kind, of every creeping thing of the ground after its kind, two of every sort shall come unto thee, to keep them alive. And take thou unto thee of all food that is eaten, and gather it to thee; and it shall be for food for thee, and for them. (Gen. 6.18-21)

In order to preserve their lives God even thought of their food. And thus this covenant reveals how loving and sensitive is God's heart towards man.

As prophesied, the flood inundated the earth. All the birds, cattle, beasts and creeping things on earth, together with all men, were drowned—save Noah's household and the living creatures which he took into the ark. God had performed according to the word in His covenant.

Having been shut within the ark for over a year, Noah and his family saw nothing but waters and heard nothing but waves. When the waters receded and they emerged from the ark, they were so frightened as to wonder if God would again visit mankind with a flood. Although they were saved, their hearts were full of fear.

We know that when God sent the flood to judge mankind He was forced into it: "Jehovah saw that the wickedness of man was great in the earth, and that every imagination of the thoughts of his heart was evil continually. And it repented Jehovah that he had made man on the earth, and it *grieved* him at his heart" (Gen. 6.5-6). Thus was God's heart revealed. In order to remove the awesome impression of the flood that was left upon people's mind and to assure them that He took no delight in destroying them, God comforted them and made known His mind to them by giving them a special proof which was in the form of a covenant.

> And God spake unto Noah, and to his sons with him, saying, And I, behold, I establish my covenant with you, and with your seed after you; and with every living creature that is with you, the birds, the cattle, and every beast of the earth with you; of all that go out of the ark, even every beast of the earth. And I will establish my covenant with you; *neither shall all flesh be cut off any more by the waters of the flood; neither shall there any more be a flood to destroy the earth*. And God said, This is the token of the covenant which I make between me and you and every living creature that is with you, for perpetual generations: I do set my bow in the cloud, and it shall be for a token of a covenant between me and the earth. And it shall come to pass, when I bring a cloud over the earth, that the bow shall be seen in the cloud, and I will remember my covenant, which is between me and you and every living creature of all flesh; and *the waters shall no more become a flood to destroy all flesh*. And the bow shall be in the cloud; and I will look upon it, that I may remember the everlasting covenant between God and

every living creature of all flesh that is upon the earth. And God said unto Noah, This is the token of the covenant which I have established between me and all flesh that is upon the earth. (Gen. 9.8–17)

In this covenant God thrice declared that there would be no more flood—so as to alleviate the fear of Noah's household and encourage them to lay hold of the words of the covenant that they might rest on it instead.

The use of a covenant is hereby made clear: In view of the lack of understanding in man of God's good will, He gives man a covenant as a pledge to hold on to. By making a covenant, He plainly informs man of His heart intention. It is as if He opens His heart to man for the latter to see what is on His heart. Oh, the Lord Creator of the heavens and earth cares so much for man that even the stones will be moved to praise!

God Enlarges Man's Faith by Covenant

Let us next review the story of God making covenant with Abraham.

Abraham displayed love, courage and purity in the double incidents of receiving back his nephew Lot and rejecting the wealth of Sodom (see Gen. 14.14–23). But afterwards God said to him, "Fear not, Abram: I am thy shield, and thy exceeding great reward" (Gen. 15.1). Thus were Abraham's inner feelings revealed: on the one hand, he could not help worrying about the four kings who might return in revenge someday; and, on the other hand, he secretly moaned over the departure of Lot, as he had no son of his own. God therefore came at just the opportune time to comfort and to strengthen him.

Nevertheless, the answer of Abraham indicated that he was not satisfied with God's promise. Said he: "O Lord Jehovah, what wilt thou give me, seeing I go childless, and he that shall be possessor of my house is Eliezer of Damascus?" (15.2) He did not realize how full of grace was God's promise. He was quite pessimistic; he had his own idea and arrangement. Yet how did God react? "Behold, the word of Jehovah came unto him, saying, This man shall not be thine heir; but he that shall come forth out of thine own bowels shall be thine heir. And he brought him forth abroad, and said, Look now toward heaven, and number the stars, if thou be able to number them: and he said unto him, So shall thy seed be" (vv. 4-5). What was it that God said to Abraham? It was a promise, not a fact. But now Abraham believed in God's promise, and this was reckoned to him for righteousness (see v.6). In believing God's promise, he became the father of faith.

After Abraham believed in the first promise, God's second promise came: "And he said unto him, I am Jehovah that brought thee out of Ur of the Chaldees, to give thee this land to inherit it" (v.7). Did Abraham believe in this promise? His capacity was too small. He voiced his doubt by asking, "O Lord Jehovah, whereby shall I know that I shall inherit it?" (v.8) This promise was too big for Abraham's faith to apprehend, so he asked God for a proof to seize upon.

Does God have any way to remedy Abraham's small faith? What did He do? God made a covenant with him (see v.18). Hence making covenant is to *supplement* that which is insufficient by promise alone. It is the best way to *deal* with unbelief, and it *enlarges* the measure of faith in man. Abraham might not be able to believe in God's promise, yet God could not alter what He had promised. For his unbelief, God established a covenant with Abraham to help him believe. God said to Abraham:

> Take me a heifer three years old, and a she-goat three years old, and a ram three years old, and a turtle-dove, and a young pigeon. And he took him all these, and divided them in the midst, and laid each half over against the other: but the birds divided he not. . . . When the sun went down, and it was dark, behold, a smoking furnace, and a flaming torch that passed between these pieces. (Gen. 15.9-10, 17)

What is the meaning of all this? This was God making covenant with Abraham. This showed that the covenant He established passed through the bowels and the blood. The bodies of these animals were divided and their blood was shed. God passed through between these pieces to insure that the covenant He made was eternally unchangeable and would never fall void.

God knew how limited was Abraham's faith. Unless He enlarged the latter's capacity to believe, nothing would be accomplished. Making covenant was therefore God's way of expanding Abraham's faith. He not only promised but also covenanted with Abraham as to what He would do. Thus did He cause Abraham to believe. For having established a covenant, God could not help but perform according to His covenant; otherwise, He would be unfaithful, unrighteous, and unlawful. Under the security of such a covenant, Abraham's capacity for faith was naturally enlarged.

God Gives Covenant to Man as Surety

Let us go further and look into the covenant which God established with David.

2 Samuel 7.4-16 and Psalm 89.19-36 speak of the same incident; except that 2 Samuel 7 does not inform us that God was establishing a covenant with David, whereas Psalm 89 clearly states that the word which Jehovah spoke to David through Nathan the prophet was a covenant. God gave His word to David and his descendants as surety. He takes pleasure in seeing men laid hold of by His word and in their requesting Him to perform accordingly. This is the very reason for giving covenant to men.

God's word to David was quite clear:

> If his children forsake my law, and walk not in mine ordinances; if they break my statutes, and keep not my commandments; then will I visit their transgression with

the rod, and their iniquity with stripes. But my loving-kindness *will I not* utterly take from him, *nor suffer* my faithfulness to fail. My covenant *will I not* break, nor alter the thing that is gone out of my lips. Once have I sworn by my holiness: I will not lie unto David: His seed shall endure for ever . . . (Ps. 89.30–36a)

All these words were in reference to God's covenant to David. Should the children of David not keep God's commandments, they would be visited with the rod; yet God could not break His covenant with David.

When was Psalm 89 written? It was written at the time when the nation of Judah was destroyed and her people were exiled to Babylon. During that particular period it seemed as though God had forgotten His covenant with David. The psalmist saw the tragic fall of the nation, so addressed God as follows: "But thou hast cast off and rejected, thou hast been wroth with thine anointed. Thou hast abhorred the covenant of thy servant: thou hast profaned his crown by casting it to the ground" (vv.38–39). Here he mentioned to God His covenant with David. Seizing upon the covenant, the psalmist questioned God: "Lord, where are thy former lovingkindnesses, which thou swarest unto David in thy faithfulness?" (v.49) Let us notice what the psalmist said here. He laid hold of the covenant and prayed. The Holy Spirit purposely records such prayer of inquiry in order to show us how much God is pleased with people who seize upon His surety and pray accordingly. Thus shall God be glorified. He takes delight in their approaching Him according to covenant, to pray or even to inquire. He enjoys their requesting Him to perform according to all His promises in the covenant.

HOW TO UTILIZE COVENANT

Having established a covenant with man, God would be unfaithful and unrighteous if he did not perform all which is written in it. We know He gives His covenant to us that we may be emboldened to inquire of Him, demanding that He would fulfill what He has said therein according to righteousness. He is now bound by the covenant; He must therefore act righteously. For this reason, all who know what a covenant is know how to pray—they may ask God with boldness. Let us illustrate this with the following instances.

Instance 1

"Hear my prayer, O Jehovah; give ear to my supplications: in thy faithfulness answer me, and in thy righteousness" (Ps. 143.1). Here David asked God to hear him not according to mercy and grace; rather, he pleaded God's faithfulness and righteousness. He did not beg; he prayed with boldness. He knew what a covenant was and knew how to lay hold of it.

Instance 2

Upon finishing the construction of the holy temple Solomon said, "Blessed be Jehovah, the God of Israel, who spake with his mouth unto David my father, and hath with his hands fulfilled it" (2 Chron. 6.4; see 2 Sam. 7.12-13). Then kneeling down before all the assembly of Israel he spread forth his hands towards heaven and prayed: ". . . Who *keepest covenant* and lovingkindness with thy servants, that walk before thee with all their heart . . . Now therefore, O Jehovah, the God of Israel, keep with thy servant David my father that which thou hast promised . . . Now therefore, O Jehovah, the God of Israel, let thy word be verified, which thou spakest unto thy servant David" (2 Chron. 6.14-17). Solomon understood that some of the things in the covenant of God with his father David had already been fullfilled, whereas others were to be continuously fulfilled; consequently, he asked God to accomplish all that He had promised in accordance with His covenant. This is praying according to covenant, seizing in prayer the surety or covenant which God has given.

Instance 3

As we observed earlier, Psalm 89 was written after the people of Israel had been taken captive to Babylon. During that period, so far as appearance went, it looked as though everything was finished, that God's promise had fallen through and that He had gone back on His covenant with David. Hence the psalmist seems to be reminding God when he asks: "Lord, where are thy former lovingkindnesses, which thou swarest unto David in thy faithfulness?" (v.49) Once again, this is praying according to covenant, laying hold of the pledge which God gives in covenant.

HOW TO KNOW GOD'S COVENANT

How can we truly know God's covenant? "The friendship of Jehovah is with them that fear him; and he will show them his covenant" (Ps. 25.14). Except God himself shows us His covenant, there is no way to know it. We may hear people talk about God's covenant, we may even understand something about it, but unless there is God's revelation we have no strength to lay hold of His word. Hence we need the Lord to give us a registration in our spirit.

What kind of persons may receive God's direction? They who fear God; because "the secret of Jehovah is with them that fear him, that he may make known his covenant to them" (same verse, Darby's translation). What is the meaning of "fear God"? To fear Him is to hallow His name—that is, to exalt Him. They who seek God's will with singleness of heart and obey Him absolutely are those who fear Him. To such as these will He tell His secret and show His covenant. People who are lazy, careless, doubtful-minded or arrogant need not expect God to reveal His secret or covenant to them. He only makes known His secret and unveils His covenant to those who fear Him. This can be attested by all who fear the Lord. For us to truly know God's covenant, we must learn to fear Him.

3 | General Remarks on the New Covenant

God has made several covenants with man. The most notable are those He established with Noah, with Abraham, with the Israelites who came out of Egypt, and also with David. There is another one He made with the children of Israel in the land of Moab besides the one He made with them in Horeb (see Deut. 29.1). But beyond all these is a covenant which God established through the Lord Jesus Christ — that which is commonly known as the New Covenant. Although there are so many covenants, the most significant ones are the Abrahamic Covenant and the New Covenant.

THE NEW COVENANT SUCCEEDS THE ABRAHAMIC COVENANT

The New Covenant expounds as well as succeeds the Abrahamic Covenant. We are shown in Galatians 3 that these two covenants run on the same line. Though the Mosaic Covenant of Law which God established with Israel stands between the Abrahamic and New Covenants (see Gal. 3.15-17), yet the Law is added because of transgressions (see Gal. 3.19; Rom. 5.20). Only the Abrahamic Covenant and the New Covenant are enacted upon promise, and, therefore, on the basis of faith (see Gal. 3.7, 9, 16-17; Heb. 8.6). They belong to the same system. In between the Abrahamic and New Covenants is the

Covenant of Law which God established with the people of Israel. This is that "first covenant" mentioned in Hebrews 8.7, which is also what we usually call the Old Covenant. The Old Covenant (or Testament) does not refer to the thirty-nine books of the Old Testament (Genesis to Malachi). Strictly speaking, the Old Covenant covers the period from Exodus 19 to the death of the Lord Jesus. The conditions for the Old Covenant are reciprocal in nature: if the children of Israel keep the Law, God will bless them; but if they violate the Law, He will punish them. This is the Old Covenant. Yet there is a covenant earlier than the Old Covenant, and that is the one God made with Abraham. Now the New Covenant is a continuation of the Abrahamic Covenant — and not of the Old Covenant.

THE FIRST COVENANT HAS FAULT

"For if that first covenant had been faultless, then would no place have been sought for a second" (Heb. 8.7). This indicates that the first one has been found faulty. So far as the covenant *itself* is concerned, "the law is holy" (Rom. 7.12), "the law is spiritual" (Rom. 7.14), "the law is good" (1 Tim. 1.8). But as to the *function* of the first covenant, "through the law cometh the knowledge of sin" (Rom. 3.20), "and the law is not of faith; but [quoting from Lev. 18.5], He that doeth them shall live in them" (Gal. 3.12). Hence this is stating that the Law demands doing good yet it fails to give the life and power to do that good. Why? Because "the law could not do, in that it was weak through the flesh" (Rom. 8.3); and therefore "by the works of the law shall no flesh be justified in his sight" (Rom. 3.20). In a word, "the law made nothing perfect" (Heb. 7.19). Thus is the Old Covenant found to be faulty.

We know that all the words from Exodus 19 to 24 are included in the covenant God made with Israel. In the third month after they were gone forth out of the land of Egypt they came into the wilderness of Sinai, and there they encamped before the Mount. Moses appeared before God and was told to say to the children of Israel: "If ye will obey my voice indeed, and keep my covenant, then ye shall be mine own possession from among all peoples: for all the earth is mine." When the people heard these words they answered together and said: "All that Jehovah hath spoken we will do" (see 19.1-8). And after Moses had proclaimed all the words of the covenant he "took the blood, and sprinkled it on the people, and said, Behold the blood of the covenant, which Jehovah hath made with you concerning all these words" (24.8).

Now in the covenant are included words such as these: "Thou shalt have no other gods before me. Thou shalt not make unto thee a graven image, nor any likeness of any thing . . . Thou shalt not bow down thyself unto them . . ." (20.3-5) Had the people of Israel kept these words? We know that even before Moses brought the tables of the testimony down from Mount Sinai the people of Israel had already made a golden calf and worshipped it in the plain (see 32.1-8). In other words, even before the tables of the testimony had reached them, the people had broken the covenant. This is the fault of the first covenant.

Were the people of Israel able to keep God's covenant afterwards? No, they were not. On the contrary, they provoked God by tempting Him and proving Him even though they witnessed His work continually for forty long years. They erred in their hearts and did not know God's ways. They saw God's work, yet they did not know His ways. This too is the fault of the first covenant.

> For finding fault with them, he saith, Behold, the days come, saith the Lord, that I will make a new covenant with the house of Israel and with the house of Judah; not according to the covenant that I made with their fathers

> in the day that I took them by the hand to lead them
> forth out of the land of Egypt; for they continued not in
> my covenant . . . (Heb. 8.8,9a)

How God expected them to continue to be faithful to His covenant! But they could not continue. In spite of their determina-
tion once made to follow the Lord, they could not follow Him
daily with faithfulness. Though they were once revived, they
were not so every day. This again is the fault of the first
covenant.

"We know that the law is spiritual: but I am carnal, sold
under sin. . . . For I know that in me, that is, in my flesh,
dwelleth no good thing: for to will is present with me, but to do
that which is good is not" (Rom. 7.14, 18). Paul's experience
proves to us that the Law itself is spiritual, but it is weak
through the flesh (Rom. 8.3). Once more, this is the fault of
the first covenant.

THE NEW COVENANT IS THE BETTER COVENANT

If the first covenant is faulty, how about the second? The
second one is the New Covenant (Heb. 8.7, 13). The New Covenant has been enacted upon a better promise (Heb. 8.6), and
it is written not on tables of stone but on tables that are hearts
of flesh (2 Cor. 3.3). Regarding this New Covenant, God puts
His laws into the mind of man and writes them on his heart
(Heb. 8.10b). In other words, with the New Covenant it is God
who both gives the charge and enables man to do His will. The
New Covenant provides us who believe with life and power to
do the good which we would desire to do, so that God may be
our God and we may be His people (Heb. 8.10c; Titus 2.14). It
also helps us to know God more deeply within ourselves, even
without the need of being instructed by men (Heb. 8.11). Consequently, it is the blood of the covenant wherewith we are
sanctified (Heb. 10.29), it is "a better covenant" (Heb. 7.22,

8.6) and "an eternal covenant" (Heb. 13.20). We want to shout Hallelujah! How sweet, how glorious, and full of grace is the New Covenant!

THE NEW COVENANT CONTAINS GOD'S PROMISE AND GOD'S FACT

We have before said that the gracious word which God gives us includes His promise, His fact, and His covenant— these three—the third of which in addition embraces the first and second. Now we intend to take a closer look at both the promise and the fact in God's covenant. The Scriptures show us that God's covenant is God's promise; except that God's promise is what He says whereas God's covenant is further interposed with an oath (Heb. 6.17). If promise is binding to God, covenant is much more binding. When God made His covenant with Abraham, He swore by himself (Heb. 6.13-14). It is further said that "God, being minded to show more abundantly unto the heirs of the promise the immutability of his counsel, interposed with an oath" (6.17). Moreover, "the Lord sware and will not repent himself" (7.21b). Therefore, God is more bound and restricted by covenant.

From the words in Hebrews 9.15-18 we are clearly to understand that there is fact as well as promise in the New Covenant: "Where a testament is, there must of necessity be the death of him that made it" (v.16). So a covenant in the Scriptures has two meanings—one is "agreement" while the other is "will" or "testament." We may therefore describe the New Covenant either as a covenant or as a testament.

God's Promise

No covenant can be instituted without promise. There is promise in every covenant. But ordinary promise gives no

surety, whereas covenantal promise undergoes a legal procedure, and is thus protected or prosecuted by law. To those who
have been deeply taught by God's grace and who know Him
well, God's promise and God's covenant do not make much
difference; for they know He is as faithful as He is righteous.
They believe that once God has promised, it shall be done.
There is no need for His promises to be put into legal form.
They look upon God's promise as being just as good as His
covenant. But to those whose faith is weak, God's covenant is
quite different from His promise, in that covenant seems to
guarantee the fulfillment of promise. Although we cannot say
all God's promises are God's covenants, we can dare to say that
all God's covenants contain His promises.

"But now hath he obtained a ministry the more excellent,
by so much as he is also the mediator of a better covenant,
which hath been enacted upon *better promises*" (Heb. 8.6).
This tells us that the New Covenant is a better covenant because it has been enacted upon better promises.

God's Fact

God's covenant contains not only promise but also will and
testament. Hebrews 9.15 speaks of "the promise of the eternal
inheritance," while verse 16 speaks of a "testament." A testament implies that something is left behind, either property or
thing. What is left behind is the fact. For example: A father
leaves a will, stating how his properties are to be distributed—
either to his son or to others. Those who inherit his inheritance
enjoy the things which he has left behind. Consequently, a
testament is not empty words; there must be fact involved.
Since a testament is also a covenant, it is logical to further conclude that there is fact in a covenant.

However, a covenant is different from God's promise and
God's fact, though it contains both. Without promise and fact
a covenant would become vain and meaningless. We thank

God, for He has joined together many promises and facts in the New Covenant. Praise the Lord, the New Covenant is so rich and perfect.

THE DISPENSATION OF THE NEW COVENANT

Before we can touch upon the dispensation of the New Covenant, we must initally decide with whom God establishes the New Covenant in the first place. Moreover, when does He make the New Covenant?

With Whom Does God Covenant?

According to the Bible, God has never made any covenant with the gentiles. The New Covenant is therefore not made with them. Since God has not previously set up any covenant with the church, how can he ever make a *second* (or New) covenant with it if there has not been a first (or Old) covenant made? With whom, then, does He establish the New Covenant? "Behold, the days come, saith Jehovah, that I will make a new covenant with *the house of Israel*, and with *the house of Judah*: not according to the covenant that I made with their fathers in the day that I took them by the hand to bring them out of the land of Egypt . . ." (Jer. 31.31-32a). When the children of Israel came out of Egypt God made a covenant with them. He now declares that He will make a new covenant with them. This distinctly informs us that God establishes the New Covenant not with the gentiles but with the house of Israel and the house of Judah.

When Is the New Covenant Made?

"Behold, the days come" (Jer. 31.31). This would indicate that at the time the words were spoken the days had not yet come. The Lord continues: "This is the covenant that I will make with the house of Israel after those days, saith Jehovah" (v.33a). According to the contents of this covenant, we believe "the days" refer to the beginning of the millennium. It is during that time that God will establish a New Covenant with the house of Israel.

How Is It That Today Is Called the Dispensation of the New Covenant?

If the New Covenant is to be established by God with the house of Israel in future days, how then can we call today the dispensation of the New Covenant? This is truly most marvelous and most gracious! On the night of His betrayal, the Lord Jesus "took a cup, and gave thanks, and gave to them, saying, Drink ye all of it; for this is my blood of the covenant . . ." (Matt. 26.27-28a—many ancient authorities insert "new" before the word "covenant"—ASV mg.). The New Covenant— oh, how musical, how marvelous, how attractive! Although we read about the New Covenant in the Old Testament book of Jeremiah, for hundreds of years afterwards nothing was ever heard of it, as though it were a forgotten treasure. During the thirty or so odd years of our Lord's earthly days He never mentioned the New Covenant. Day after day, year after year, He made no reference to it. How then did it happen that when He was having supper with the disciples He at this particular time took the cup, blessed it, and gave it to them, saying, "Drink ye all of it; for this is my blood of the new covenant"? He not only mentioned the New Covenant but even stated that "this is my blood of the new covenant."

O holy and gracious Lord, we worship You with tears of gratitude and praise You with tears of joy! How full of life and full of riches is the New Covenant. To those who know You not, it is but letter. But Lord, You know what it is, and You have unveiled it this day. You have opened the heavenly spiritual treasure-house and distributed its treasures to Your beloved ones. Lord, this is indeed most marvelous and most gracious! We want to thank and praise You once more.

Due to the exceeding greatness of the grace of the Lord, this New Covenant is now applicable to all the redeemed people. Though it shall be after those days that God will make a new covenant with the house of Israel and the house of Judah, yet all the redeemed ones may enjoy it beforehand since the Lord has paid the price with His blood. This is just the same as our being justified by faith as Abraham was justified by faith, even though God made his covenant with Abraham and not with us.

We are today being put under the New Covenant which God has promised Israel some day to enjoy because the Lord Jesus has already shed His blood—even the blood of the New Covenant. The Lord is building us up with the principle of the New Covenant. He blesses us with the blessings of the New Covenant. We know the Lord Jesus shed His blood not only for the remission of sin but also for the establishment of the New Covenant. For remission of sin is only a process, a way to the goal. The purpose of the shedding of the blood is to establish the New Covenant. Atonement is related to the institution of the New Covenant in that without the problem of sin solved the blessing of the New Covenant can not come upon us. Thank the Lord, His blood solves the problem of sin and inaugurates the New Covenant. For this reason, this age is truly the dispensation of the New Covenant. How we praise God for it!

THE CONTENTS OF THE NEW COVENANT

What are the contents of the New Covenant? We shall give a general outline now, and develop its various aspects later on.

> For this is the covenant that I will make with the house of
> Israel after those days, saith the Lord; I will put my laws

into their mind, and on their heart also will I write them:
and I will be to them a God, and they shall be to me a
people: and they shall not teach every man his fellow-
citizen, and every man his brother, saying, Know the
Lord: for all shall know me, from the least to the greatest
of them. For I will be merciful to their iniquities, and
their sins will I remember no more. (Heb. 8.10-12)

This passage of the Bible tells us clearly that the New Covenant
contains three main parts:

(1) God will put His laws into our minds and write them on
our hearts so that He may be our God and we may be His people. In this, God enters into men and unites himself with them
in life.

(2) Being in us, this law shall enable us to know God
without need of being taught by others. This is knowing God
inwardly.

(3) God will be merciful to our iniquities and remember
not our sins. This is forgiveness of sin.

Hebrews 8.10-11 forms a unit, while verse 12 makes a new
start. With the conjunction "For" heading verse 12, we would
understand that the forgiveness of sin is something already
done. Speaking from God's side, verses 10 and 11 reveal His
purpose, and hence they are stated first; whereas verse 12 is
declared second because it relates to God's process towards arriving at His purpose. But speaking from the viewpoint of our
spiritual experience, God forgives our iniquities and remembers not our sins before He puts His laws into our mind and
writes them on our heart that He may be our God and we may
be His people who know Him in a deeper way.

Concerning these main parts of the New Covenant, we may
list them as follows:

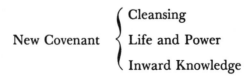

The New Covenant meets our needs perfectly. There is no necessity to add anything to it, nor is there the possibility of subtracting something from it. What God has done is just too perfect. In saving us, He gives us these three magnificent blessings in the Lord Jesus. Having the New Covenant, we have cleansing, life and power, and also inward knowledge of God. May we all say, How perfect and glorious is the New Covenant, How graciously has God treated us!

4 | The Surety of the New Covenant

"This is my blood of the [new] covenant, which is poured out for many unto remission of sins" (Matt. 26.28 mg.). This verse indicates that the blood of Christ is the blood of the New Covenant. This blood is shed especially for the establishment of the covenant. In other words, the New Covenant is inaugurated by blood; consequently, it is trustworthy and secure.

THE NECESSITY OF THE BLOOD

Why must the New Covenant be initiated by blood? Why is this covenant effective only if it is inaugurated with blood? To understand this we need to retrace the story of the garden of Eden to recognize the demand of the Law.

We know that when Adam was driven out of the garden of Eden he lost life and inheritance as well as the position of having fellowship with God. Death reigned from Adam until Moses (Rom. 5.14). Sin and death reigned from Moses until Christ (Rom. 5.21). This does not mean that from Adam to Moses there was no sin. The Bible tells us that "until the law sin was in the world; but sin is not imputed when there is no law" (Rom. 5.13). At Mount Sinai Moses received the covenant of law from God. And that covenant was conditional: if the people kept its words they would be blessed; if not, they would be cursed (Gal. 3.12, 10). Why, then, was the Law given to them?

Because "through the law cometh the knowlege of sin" (Rom. 3.20) that they might be "kept in ward under the law" (Gal. 3.23). In this respect they were under the dominion of sin as they once before were under the dominion of death.

Before Christ came into the world human beings suffered two great losses: first, the loss which came from Adam having sinned; and second, the loss which came from our inability to keep the law of God. With death and sin ruling, we are thus separated from God and cannot enjoy His presence. We become foolish and know not God. We do not possess the spiritual life and power to do God's will. Alas, in Adam and under the law we have nothing whereof to boast except to cry out: "Wretched man that I am! Who shall deliver me out of sin and death?" Is there no way to solve the problems of sin and death? Indeed there is: in shedding His blood, the Lord Jesus has solved both problems. Because of His shed blood we need not die and our sins are being cleansed.

Originally God had designed to give to us His own life and all things pertaining to godliness. Due to our sin and the death which comes from sin, we became alienated from God, unable to obtain all that belongs to Him. We lost what God had already given and what He had intended yet to give us. But now the blood of the Lord Jesus cleanses us of our sin and restores .our relationship with God (Eph. 2.13), so that whatever He has given or will yet give may come to us without any hindrance. Hence the blood of the Lord Jesus not only reconciles us to God (Col. 1.20), it also gives us God himself (Rom. 8.32).

The blood of Christ has accomplished the work of redemption, even that of eternal redemption. The blood of bulls and goats upon which the people in the dispensation of the Old Covenant depended only caused them to recall their sins year by year (Heb. 10. 3, 4); but Christ who with His own blood entered in once for all into the holiest place has obtained eternal redemption (Heb. 9.12). His blood has so cleansed our conscience (Heb. 9.14) that we have no more consciousness of sins (Heb. 10.2). Thank God, the blood of Christ has perfectly solved the problem of sin forever.

Through the shedding of the blood of Christ we now have the remission of sins (Heb. 9.22; Matt. 26.28; Eph. 1.7). To know this fact is glorious indeed. All who are sensitive to the shame and hatefulness of sin appreciate this. How we thank God that the blood of the Lord Jesus has not only solved the problems of sin and death but also restored all which we had lost as well as added to us what we had never had before. The blood has done a most marvelous work, which is, that it gives us God.

Hence the blood of the Lord Jesus not only atones for our sins that we may not be penalized, but in addition it restores completely all that was lost in the garden of Eden as well as gives us many new things. "This cup," said the Lord, "is the new covenant in my blood" (Luke 22.20). The Lord's blood is therefore shed on the one hand for the remission of sins — which negatively speaking takes away all that is harmful to us, and is shed on the other hand for the inauguration of the New Covenant — which positively speaking restores our lost heritage and gives us new things too. The blood of the Lord is for both atonement and restoration.

THE RELATION BETWEEN BLOOD AND COVENANT

What is the relation between blood and covenant? We may say that blood is the foundation while covenant is the document. The blood lays the foundation of the covenant and the covenant reveals the document established in the blood. Without the blood no covenant can be inaugurated, nor will it be effective. God enumerates in the covenant all the inheritance He is giving us, and this covenant He seals with the blood of the Lord Jesus. It is on the ground of this New Covenant of the blood of the Lord Jesus that we come into our spiritual inheritance.

On this account the New Covenant is an absolutely legal document. It is made wholly according to the righteous procedure of God. It is not merely the spoken word of God, but is a kind of document which He has drawn up through the blood of Christ. As we may know concerning the salvation of God, whatever is done before the crucifixion of the Lord Jesus is done by God's grace, but anything done after the crucifixion of the Lord Jesus is done by His righteousness.

This does not mean that after the Lord's crucifixion there is no more grace; it simply suggests that as water is to a pipe, so the grace of God is now flowing to us through the channel of righteousness: "As sin reigned in death, even so might grace reign through righteousness unto eternal life through Jesus Christ our Lord" (Rom. 5.21). Grace reigns through righteousness. God not only gives us grace, He also gives that grace through righteousness. This is God's grace—that He loved us and sent His Son the Lord Jesus to die for us. If He did not love us He would not be gracious, nor would the Lord Jesus come to accomplish the work of atonement. But after the Lord Jesus has died for us and the work of redemption is finished, it is God's righteousness which saves us if we believe in the Lord.

Never can we say that God has no grace. For if He does not have grace there would be no New Covenant. Yet should all which God gives us be built solely on grace, our faith may falter, because grace may one day cease since it has not undergone any legal process. Thank God, not only does He have grace, but also His grace is expressed in a covenant. In order to be gracious to us God binds himself with a covenant. We may say that grace appears in the guise of righteousness. Such righteousness does not eliminate grace; on the contrary, it is the highest expression of grace.

What we receive is God's grace; nonetheless, God has

established His covenant with us through the blood so that on the basis of that covenant we may ask Him to treat us according to His righteouness. We indeed are now standing on the ground of grace, yet this grace is communicated to us through righteousness. The blood of Christ has become the righteous foundation by which God's covenant with us can *never* fail. So when we approach God on the ground of the blood and of righteousness, He cannot but fulfill towards us all that is in the covenant.

One who is well experienced in the Lord has observed that "God's covenant is a treatment for unbelief; He uses covenant to cure the unbelieving." For example, in order to obtain the forgiveness of sin someone might pray till he obtains peace in his heart as evidence of forgiveness. Yet the word of God actually declares: "If we confess our sins, he is faithful and righteous to forgive us our sins, and to cleanse us from all unrighteousness" (1 John 1.9). One thing must be observed, and that is, whether we have *confessed* our sins. The confession spoken of here does not of course apply to what is done carelessly or is void of any repugnant feeling towards sin. Not at all. Here, it is a confession which arises from seeing and condemning sin as sin under the light and is openly acknowledged before God. We confess and God forgives. If we confess our sins we should believe that He has forgiven us, and thus we have perfect peace in our heart.

One brother has put it this way: "If you do your part, will not God do His?" This word is truly most meaningful. The question is, Have you confessed your sins? If you really have, you need only believe in God's word—disregarding how you feel, what others may say, or what thought Satan may inject into your mind.

For this reason, the Christian life is lived by laying hold of God's word, trusting that He is faithful and righteous. Whatever He says, so is it. If we wholly stand on the covenant which the Lord Jesus has set, God will take care of us. He will perform all that is in the covenant, for He has already accepted the blood of the Lord Jesus. Since God has attached His will to the covenant, he can only move within His covenant. Had God not made a covenant with us He would be free to treat us as He likes; but since He has established a covenant with us, God must perform according to its words; for He cannot be unrighteous. We thank God for loving us and being compassionate towards us to such an extent that He treats us according to righteousness. Oh! Can there be greater grace than this?

We may say that without the blood of the Lord Jesus we do not deserve anything; through His blood, though, we shall have everything. By His blood we now have the right to enjoy all that is in the covenant. When we come by the blood of the Lord Jesus and ask God to bless us according to His covenant, He will most certainly do so because He cannot be unrighteous. This New Covenant is established in the blood of the Lord. He has already paid the price. We are but asking God to grant us what is in the covenant according to the value of blood in His sight. One brother has well said: "No one knows just how much the blood means." We do not comprehend the value of blood; even so, we do not need to evaluate it according to our judgment. We only need to ask God to treat us in accordance with the value of the blood in His sight and the covenant which is sealed by that blood. We may approach Him, saying, "I want this because You are the God of covenant." Our God will never fail, nor will he ever break His covenant.

The blood of the New Covenant has solved our problem of sins, removed the obstacle between us and God, restored our lost heritage, and granted us every spiritual blessing in the heavenlies regarding life and godliness (Eph. 2.12, 13, 18, 19; 1.3; 2 Peter 1.3). Whatever is recorded in the New Covenant is our blessed portion through the blood. According to Hebrews 8.10-12, the New Covenant includes three precious parts: cleansing, life and power, and inward knowledge (to be discussed in detail in Chapters 6-8 below). The reason we do not know how to deal with God according to the words of the covenant lies in our lack of understanding as to how much blessing the blood has gained for us. May we always remember that every spiritual blessing and spiritual inheritance comes from the covenant of the blood. The blood is the foundation of this New Covenant.

Hence when we ask according to covenant we are not asking for things which do not belong to us, rather are we claiming what is reserved for us in God (1 Peter 1.3, 4). Praying according to covenant is not praying without ground; it is instead reclaiming for ourselves what has already been given us in the covenant. As we ask according to covenant God must stand on our side because of the covenant. For this reason, often when we come to God according to the New Covenant of the blood, we "claim" instead of "ask." This certainly does not suggest we do not need to pray today. What is really meant here is that in today's prayer the element of "claiming" should exceed that of "asking."

A brother who knows God well once declared that "since Calvary, all the 'ask' in the Bible should be changed to 'take'. " To this word all who know God—who know Calvary and the blood—will respond with an amen. Let us ever be mindful that through the blood we claim what is rightfully ours. We shall persist in stating that the current principle of God's dealing with us is according to His righteousness as well as His grace. Whatever is granted us in the New Covenant is now our right. In full accordance with His righteouness, God cannot fail to give us all that is recorded in the covenant if we claim it.

Sometimes it may appear that God has forgotten His covenant. During such times we may remind Him of His covenant. "Put me in remembrance," says the Lord (Is. 43.26). He wishes us to remind Him. There are times when we may reverently say to Him: "God, please remember Your covenant, remember the words You have promised. Do according to Your promised words; fulfill in me Your covenant." If we so ask and believe, we shall not fail to receive.

A GREAT PRAYER

> Now the God of peace, who brought again from the dead the great shepherd of the sheep with the blood of an *eternal covenant*, even our Lord Jesus, make you perfect in every good thing to do his will, working in us that which is well-pleasing in his sight, through Jesus Christ; to whom be the glory for ever and ever. Amen. (Heb. 13.20, 21)

This is a prayer of faith as well as being a great prayer in the Bible. The writer of Hebrews prays that according to the blood of the eternal covenant God will cause Jesus Christ whom He has raised from the dead to dwell in us that we may do His will and walk in His pleasure. This further shows us how this prayer of faith—this great prayer—is offered up on the ground of the covenant affirmed by the shed blood of the Lord. We ought to have the faith to lay hold of the covenant and pray accordingly. By the covenant we should ask Him: "Oh God, I ask You according to Your covenant." Such prayer is powerful; such faith is effective. Confidence in the covenant increases our courage to approach God.

May we all remember that we have the right to pray according to covenant. We may ask God to act according to His covenant. But if there is no faith, our prayer will be of no avail. God has reserved everything in the New Covenant in just the way a person deposits his money in a bank. If the person believes, he can draw it out continually.

Since the New Covenant is inaugurated by the blood of the Lord Jesus, it is most trustworthy. Our God has restricted himself by the covenant. He so condescends himself to make covenant with us that we may believe in Him and draw nigh to

Him. He gives us a tangible document by which we may pray to Him. Let us therefore sing with boldness:

> *Standing on the promises I shall not fall,*
>   *List'ning ev'ry moment to the Spirit's call.*
> *Resting in my Savior as my All in all,*
>   *Standing on the promises of God.*
>
> *Standing, Standing,*
>   *Standing on the promises of God my Savior;*
> *Standing, Standing,*
>   *I'm standing on the promises of God.*
>   —R. KELSO CARTER

We will furthermore declare with joy:

> *How firm a foundation, ye saints of the Lord,*
>   *Is laid for your faith in His excellent Word!*
> *What more can He say than to you He hath said,*
>   *To you who for refuge to Jesus have fled?*
>   —G. KEITH

5 | The New Covenant and Testament

In the third chapter, in the discussion about the promise and the fact of the New Covenant, we mentioned that the word "testament" in Hebrews 9.16 is the same Greek word translated "covenant." In the book of Hebrews there are a number of places which speak of the covenant. We may say that one of the objectives of Hebrews is to tell us what the New Covenant really is. Chapters 6 through 13 are especially devoted to this subject. Presently we shall describe the relationship between the New Covenant and testament.

> For this cause he is the mediator of a new covenant, that a death having taken place for the redemption of the transgressions that were under the first covenant, they that have been called may receive the promise of the eternal inheritance. For where a testament is, there must of necessity be the death of him that made it. For a testament is of force where there hath been death: for it doth never avail while he that made it liveth. (Heb. 9.15-17)

Aside from its basic and most obvious meaning, the word "mediator" in verse 15 also meant in the Greek original, "one who acts as a guarantee so as to secure something which otherwise would not be obtained."* Hence it may likewise be rendered as

---

*The author's explanation of the Greek original is best expressed in the definition given by W.E. Vine in his *An Expository Dictionary of New Testament Words* (Old Tappen, N.J.: Fleming H. Revell Co., 1966 ed.), III, p. 55 — *Translator*

"executor." The word "testament" in verses 16 and 17 is in the Greek original the same word translated "covenant." Thus this passage of Scripture tells us of four important things: (1) the fact that a covenant is also a testament, (2) the testator, (3) the executor, and (4) the testament in force.

COVENANT IS ALSO TESTAMENT

Why is covenant also testament? Who makes covenant with us—the Lord Jesus or God? According to God's word it is God and not the Lord Jesus who covenants with us. God is the other party to the covenant. Nevertheless, the Lord Jesus is the One who concludes the covenant, since it is inaugurated by His blood. From God's standpoint it is a covenant, because He covenants or enters into agreement with us. But from the standpoint of the Lord Jesus it is a testament, because He has died that we may receive the promise of the eternal inheritance (Heb. 9.15). A covenant is valid without the need of the death of the covenanter, but a testament cannot be in force until the death of the testator. Therefore, it is God who covenants with us, and through the death of the Lord Jesus we receive the inheritance inscribed in the testament.

So far as the contents are concerned, the New Covenant and Testament are exactly the same. They are alike also in regard to the inheritance we inherit. The only difference lies in the way of approach—whether done so from God's side or from the side of the Lord Jesus. According to the covenant which God has made with us, it is God who forgives our sins that we may be cleansed, who gives us life and power, and who imparts to us an inward knowledge that we may know Him in a deeper way. According to the testament that the Lord Jesus has left to us, it is the Lord Jesus who leaves with us cleansing, life and power, and the knowledge of God.

THE LORD JESUS THE TESTATOR

As we have mentioned before, the New Covenant was prophesied at the time of Jeremiah. Yet for several hundred years thereafter it seemed to be totally overlooked. Suddenly one day, that is, on the night of His betrayal, the Lord Jesus "took bread; and when he had given thanks, he brake it, and said, This is my body, which is for you . . . In like manner also the cup, after supper, saying, This cup is the new covenant in my blood" (1 Cor. 11.23-25). This New Covenant is that most glorious new covenant mentioned in the book of Jeremiah. Now, through the blood of the Lord Jesus, it has become our inheritance which we may freely enjoy. This indicates that the New Covenant is our Lord's testament and that He is the testator. In His testament He has given us the spiritual inheritance which is included in the New Covenant as described in Hebrews 8.10-12. Whatever is obtained through the testament is not anything that the believer originally has, nor can it be the result of his own work, because it is all left to him by the Lord Jesus.

THE LORD JESUS THE EXECUTOR

Our Lord is not only the testator, He is also the executor. As we have said before, His being the mediator of the New Covenant means that He is in addition the executor. In writing a will it is important to have witnesses, but it is even more important to have an executor. A testament will lie in waste if there is none who can execute it.

We thank God, for the Lord Jesus is both testator and executor. He is the testator by death and the executor by resurrection. He brought the blood into the holiest place (Heb. 9.12), thus signifying that the testator has died. He is now in heaven acting as the mediator of the New Covenant, thereby proving that He has the power of an executor. Oh, how worthy is our Lord to be praised! "Now hath he obtained a ministry the more excellent, by so much as he is also the mediator of a better covenant" (Heb. 8.6).

> Ye are come unto mount Zion, and unto the city of the living God, the heavenly Jerusalem, and to innumerable hosts of angels, to the general assembly and church of the firstborn who are enrolled in heaven, and to God the Judge of all, and to the spirits of just men made perfect, and to Jesus the mediator of a new covenant, and to the blood of sprinkling that speaketh better than that of Abel. (Heb. 12.22-24)

We are not come to a mount that may be touched (v.18), rather are we come to Mount Zion—the place where God, the angels, the just men who have been resurrected, and the church of the firstborn all assemble. Here is also the Lord Jesus, the mediator of the New Covenant. He is in heaven not only as high priest but also as mediator. He serves as the executor of the covenant to put the New Covenant in force. He shall see the fruit of the covenant of His blood in that we will have the life and power to obey God, the ability to know Him in a deeper way, and peace in our conscience through the forgiveness of sins. He is the guarantor of all these things. According to God's faithfulness and righteousness, this covenant will never fail nor be broken. According to the power of the Lord's resurrection it is forever effective. Hallelujah! the Lord leaves us a rich inheritance, and He has the power to enforce His testament!

THE TESTAMENT IN FORCE

"Where a testament is, there must of necessity be the death of him that made it. For a testament is of force where there hath been death . . ." (Heb. 9.16,17a) One day our Lord said, "This cup is the new covenant in my blood" (Luke 22.20). This is asserting that the testator is dead and that therefore the covenant commences to be in force. Having brought His blood into the holiest place (Heb. 9.12), the Lord Jesus declares to God that the testator has died. We, the living, also know that the testator has died. For as often as we eat the bread and drink the cup we proclaim the Lord's death (1 Cor. 11.26). The testator having died, the testament is now in force.

It is the responsibility of the executor to enforce the testament. Every item in the testament is ours. If the executor is faithful we shall possess all of them. If he should be unfaithful we shall be deprived of our full share. Since our Lord is the executor we will no doubt have all that is in the testament. What He has left to us contains three parts; namely, cleansing, life and power, and deeper knowledge of God—and these supply all our needs in spiritual life. Having died and risen for us, the Lord Jesus becomes the responsible executor as well as the testator. Accordingly, we should no longer live a life of poverty, barrenness and weakness. We ought to claim all that is in the testament.

Have we ever considered why baptism is once-for-all, whereas breaking of bread in remembrance of the Lord must be frequently done? Why, in the apostolic age, did believers remember the Lord in the breaking of bread on the first day of the week? Because the cup is the cup of the New Covenant (Luke 22.20, 1 Cor. 11.25). As we drink the cup each Lord's day we know we are standing in relationship to the covenant. "This cup is the new covenant in my blood." As often as we drink of it we do not see the physical produce of the vine, we instead see the new covenant of the blood of our Lord. He wants us to drink all which He has given us. Each Lord's day we review this New Covenant that we may once again remember the Lord and take whatever is included in the cup.

How the Lord desires us to remember that God, being

bound by the covenant, is most willing to give us everything promised therein. He expects us never to forget that all things in the New Covenant are for us permanently to enjoy. Whenever we come before God to remember the Lord, we are reminded of these things. The bread is for remembering the Lord; the cup is also for remembering the Lord. He always treats us according to the conditions laid down in the covenant. For this reason, when we remember the Lord, we remember Him in the covenant.

True, the effectiveness of the testament is not dependent upon our effort; nevertheless, it is quite consequential whether or not we know the richness of the testament, believe in the force of the testament, and trust the Lord Jesus as its executor. Let us illustrate this by what follows.

Sample 1   *Forgiveness of Sin*

In the matter of forgiveness of sin, one fancies that he has to try his best to do good in order to obtain forgiveness; but he has no idea as to how many years of good works he must do. Another imagines he needs to keep on praying until one day he thinks he has got peace. We must say, though, that these efforts are done in and of themselves, and not given by the testament.

We know we cannot compensate for sins by good works, for it is simply our duty to do good anyway. Neither can we petition God to forget our sins, because such request is not able to cancel these criminal cases before Him. Nor can we pray till we forget our sins and thus regain peace. The only way to have them forgiven and cleansed is through the *blood*. "Apart from shedding of blood there is no remission" (Heb. 9.22). It is the blood of the Lord Jesus that solves the problem of our sins. It is His blood which cleanses us from all our iniquities (1 John 1.7). For "if we confess our sins, he is faithful and righteous to forgive us our sins, and to cleanse us from all unrighteousness" (1 John 1.9). This is the testament, this is the New Covenant. Do we believe?

Sample 2   *Deliverance from Sin*

"Sin shall not have dominion over you: for ye are not under law, but under grace" (Rom. 6.14). Someone will argue that in spite of what the Bible has said he is still weak as water and fails whenever tempted. Such a one will doubtless be struggling all the time. It is he himself who is trying. This is not the New Covenant nor inheritance from the testament. Should he see what the testament really is, he would say: "Thank God, the power is not from me, but is given by the Lord." This is the testament, this is the New Covenant. Do we believe?

Sample 3   *Knowing and Doing God's Will*

One will ask how he can know the will of God and do it. We will answer that the knowledge of His will and the power to perform it are left to us through the testament of the Lord Jesus. Each one who belongs to the Lord must do God's will. And he is able both to know and to do His will, for the Lord's testament has granted us both (Heb. 13.20,21). This is the testament, this is the New Covenant. Do we believe?

The eternal inheritance which our Lord has left to us is spiritual. It is inexhaustible. We may draw from it endlessly. Yet how many of the Lord's people today have their conscience cleansed and thus have no more consciousness of sins (Heb. 10.2)? How many can say that having the laws of the Lord put in their minds and written on their hearts they are able to do God's will and please Him by the life and power within them? How many can testify that with the Lord's anointing in them they know Him without the need of being instructed by people? We ought to know that the Lord has made the New Covenant in His blood. He has not only left to us rich inheritance, He himself also serves as the executor of this testament. If we claim it by faith we shall experience much abundance and liberty.

O Lord, cause us to see Your testament and New Covenant that Your heart may be satisfied with the effect of the covenant of the blood.

6 | The Characteristics of the New Covenant: (1) Cleansing

We shall now focus our attention on a discussion of the characteristics of the New Covenant. As we have said before, the New Covenant is composed of three main parts as indicated in Hebrews 8.10-12. Speaking from the viewpoint of God's eternal purpose, He first gives us His life and power that He may be our God and we may be His people in the law of life, thus enabling us to know Him in a deeper inward way and to live Him out in our daily walk. Forgiveness of sin is but a procedure by which to reach His end; it is therefore listed last in the Scripture. But speaking from the point of view of our spiritual experience, we always have cleansing first (the cleansing which comes from the forgiveness of sin), and then we become God's people in the law of life, knowing Him more inwardly. In our present discussion we will begin with the forgiveness of sin.

Hebrews 8.10-11 is all of one breath, whereas verse 12 forms another. According to the original Greek text this latter verse commences with the word "For" — "For I will be merciful to their iniquities, and their sins will I remember no more" — indicating that God forgives and forgets our sins before he gives us life. In other words, the thing mentioned in verse 12 occurs prior to the things cited in verses 10 and 11. And so we shall look first into how our sins are forgiven and cleansed according to the New Covenant.

THE TWO ASPECTS OF SIN

From the scriptural viewpoint sin is composed of two aspects: sinful nature and sinful act. Sinful nature is the sin which dwells in man, that which reigns within, controlling and directing him to commit sin (Rom. 6.17, 7.20, 21). Sinful act is the sin which is manifested without, that which is committed in the daily life of man. Every sinful act of ours—whether small or big, hidden or presumptuous—constitutes a guilty case before God and is simultaneously condemned by Him (Rom. 1.32, 6.23). This causes us to feel ill-at-ease in our conscience each time we remember it. As we struggle in vain against the sin which rules in us, we feel frustrated and wretched (Rom. 7.23, 24). Sinful act, therefore, needs to be forgiven and cleansed; sinful nature needs to be delivered and emancipated from (Rom. 6.7, 22).

Thank God, the blood of the Lord Jesus has dealt with our guilt before God and cleansed our conscience (Matt. 26.28, Rev. 1.5, Heb. 9.14), and the cross of the Lord Jesus has dealt with our old man that we may be delivered and set free from the power of sin (Rom. 6.6, 18). Romans 1-5.11 refers to our sins before God, and so the blood is mentioned; while Romans 5.12-8.39 focuses on the sin within us, and accordingly, what is there emphasized is the cross on which our old man was crucified with Christ that the body of sin may be unemployed so that we should no longer be in bondage to sin.

SINS NEED TO BE FORGIVEN

No one who is truly awakened spiritually is unconscious of his sins. Like the prodigal son of Luke 15, he becomes aware, at the moment when he comes to himself, that he has sinned against his father as well as heaven. A person who is enlightened by the Holy Spirit will not fail to reprove himself for his sins (John 16.8). This is the time when he needs God's forgiveness. If he does not see his sin, he will not seek forgiveness. But once he notices it, he will spontaneously think of his guilt before God, the penalty of sin, the ceaseless suffering of hell, and the hope of salvation. Then and there is the gospel preached to us, proclaiming that the Lord Jesus has died on the cross and His blood has been poured out for the remission of sins (Matt. 26.28). By His blood our sins are washed away (Rev. 1.5). Upon hearing and believing the gospel we shall receive the remission of sins (Acts 10.43, 26.18) and the cleansing of our conscience (Heb. 9.14).

In Luke 7.36-50 we are shown that the forgiveness of God meant little to a self-righteous Simon, while it was greatly appreciated by a sinner who was criticized with the epithet: "What manner of woman this is"! This sinful woman had continually incurred the mockery and disdain of men, plunging her into self-shame. Yet here was Jesus who—so holy yet so approachable—permitted her to stand behind Him and weep at His feet. She wept as a means of pouring forth her agony due to sinning; she wept to discharge the hidden things in her heart; she wept to complain that there was no deliverer; and she wept to express her hope for a Savior. However, her weeping did not gain Simon's sympathy; it instead precipitated his silent criticism (v.39). Indeed, the tears of sorrow for sin was something a self-righteous Simon could never understand. But this Jesus understood! He first corrected Simon and then testified for the weeping woman, saying, "Her sins which are many are forgiven" (v.47a). Later He told her, "Thy sins are forgiven. . . . Thy faith hath saved thee; go in peace" (vv.48-50). To her this forgiveness is a great gospel! For this forgiveness takes away her secret sorrow and gives her peace. This forgiveness has become a gospel to many great sinners ever since.

In Mark 2.1-12 we are told that to those self-righteous scribes the forgiveness of God was but empty reasoning, because they judged the Son of God wrongly for His authority to forgive (vv.6-7). Yet it was actual healing to the palsied man borne by four friends. Alas, how often sin damages man's body as well as causes pain to the heart. We readily acknowledge that many sicknesses are attributable to natural reasons, such as infection or over-exhaustion. But the Bible also reveals that some sicknesses are the consequences of sin (Mark 2.5, John 5.14). If a sickness is due to sin, whether hidden or manifested, the sinner certainly knows about it. What can he say and do except express regret and to mourn. In the case of the palsied man, the Lord knew the cause of this particular sickness. So that first He said to the man sick of the palsy, "Son, thy sins are forgiven" (v.5), and then spoke once more to him and said: "Arise, take up thy bed, and go unto thy house" (v.11). What a tremendous gospel this is! Such forgiveness as this has forever afterwards become a great gospel to all who are sick through sin.

THE TRUSTWORTHINESS OF FORGIVENESS

According to the experience of those who serve the Lord, the more that people see sin through God's enlightenment the more they are sorrowful for their sins, and the more they appreciate the grace of forgiveness. Yet there are people who always fear that God will not forgive because of the greatness of their sins, both in number and in gravity. Some may have received forgiveness, but their conscience has been so weakened by sin that its every recollection will bring in the fear of not being pardoned. Nay, they even go so far as to surmise that forgiveness will be too cheap should God really forgive them. All who embrace such wrong attitudes need to know the trustworthiness of forgiveness, for it is not without firm foundation. They would recognize the following two points.

Forgiveness Is Based on the Righteousness of God

Our God is a holy God (1 Peter 1.16). He loves righteousness and hates iniquity (Heb. 1.9). His holy nature cannot bear with sin; His righteous attitude cannot but judge iniquity. His word clearly states: "The wages of sin is death" (Rom. 6.23); and, "Apart from shedding of blood there is no remission" (Heb. 9.22b). Since we have sinned, God will have to condemn us. According to His nature He is holy, therefore He cannot tolerate sin. According to His working procedure He is righteous, hence He cannot but punish sin. According to His own Self He is glorious, hence sinners who dare to approach Him must die. God has to deal with us according to the principle of His holiness, righteousness, and glory. And so, our sins will not be forgiven without passing through God's judgment. God will not overlook our crime. He forgives our sins and remembers not our unrighteousness only because of the blood of the Lord Jesus (Matt. 26.28, Eph. 1.7).

Grace never reigns by itself, it reigns through righteousness (Rom. 5.21). Grace does not come directly to us, it comes to us indirectly through the cross. God does not forgive our sins because He pities us when He sees us repent, express regret, exhibit sorrow, and weep. No, God can never forgive on that basis. He must first judge our sins and then He forgives (Is. 53.5,10,12).

A common notion held by many is that "grace and righteousness cannot both be preserved." Yet all who have been taught by grace will declare that in forgiving our sins God has kept both grace and righteousness intact. This is not only true with God, even His redeemed ones will sometimes reflect, in shadow, this marvelous harmony. Once a high school girl told this story: Her principal belonged to the Lord. Once someone broke some school furniture. The principal investigated the case, but no one would confess. She therefore instructed the students on the unrighteousness of destroying school furniture, but even more so on the cowardice of not confessing. She wept as she talked. Finally, one student stood up and confessed, but she did not have the means to repay the damage. So the principal paid it with her own money and forgave the student at the same time. Such an act of grace through righteousness caused this student to know grace and righteousness as well as sin.

Oh how the holy Lord, on that day when He bore the sin of the world on the cross, cried out: "My God, my God, why hast thou forsaken me?" (Matt. 27.46b) This was far more painful to Him than was the thorny crown on His head and the scourging wounds in His body. "He was wounded for our transgressions, he was bruised for our iniquities" (Is. 53.5a). Who can say forgiveness is cheap? All who have been taught by grace will sing with tears of gratefulness:

> *The depth of all Thy suffering*
> *No heart could e'er conceive,*
> *The cup of wrath o'erflowing*
> *For us Thou didst receive;*
> *And, oh, of God forsaken*
> *On the accursed tree;*
> *With grateful hearts, Lord Jesus,*
> *We now remember Thee.*
> — GEORGE W. FRASER

Forgiveness Is Characteristic of the New Covenant

Let us read again Hebrews 8.12—"For I will be merciful to their iniquities, and their sins will I remember no more." This is one of the blessed portions given to us in the New Covenant. It speaks of God in Christ forgiving our sins. Because Christ has shed His blood for us, God is able to be merciful toward our iniquities. He not only forgives them but also remembers them no more. He can forget our sins, not because He has over-looked them nor because He has tried not to remember, but because the blood of Christ has blotted out our transgressions and washed our sins away (Is. 44.22, Heb. 1.3, Rev. 1.5). God has today bound himself within a covenant, and He will gladly be restricted by it. When He says He will be merciful to our in-iquities, He will unquestionably be merciful. When he says He will no more remember our sins, He will most certainly not re-member. This is the New Covenant. This is the gospel.

How regrettable that we often forget what God remembers and remember what God forgets. Some people are always mus-ing: Does God really forgive after I have committed so many grievous sins? Will He indeed remember them no more? Yet others may think that even though God has blotted out sins, the scars which no doubt remain will forever remind God of what a sinner they are. All who entertain such thoughts know nothing of the New Covenant and are therefore unable to en-joy its privileges.

Let us remember well that in forgiving our sins and forget-ting our unrighteousness God is simply fulfilling the very first item of the New Covenant. In making the covenant God declares: "I will be merciful to their iniquities, and their sins will I remember no more." In case He fails to forgive our sins we may register our claim with Him, saying, "O God, You have covenanted with us, You are obligated to forgive our sins, You must act according to Your covenant." Since He has estab-lished the covenant, He will certainly perform accordingly. He is no longer free to forgive or not to forgive as He pleases, because He has deliberately given us the surety of a covenant.

> The law having a shadow of the good things to come, not the very image of the things, can never with the same sac-rifices year by year, which they offer continually, make perfect them that draw nigh. Else would they not have ceased to be offered? because the worshippers, having

been once cleansed, would have had no more consciousness of sins. (Heb. 10.1-2)

This means that by offering the same sacrifices of the blood of
bulls and goats the worshippers were unable to obtain the
peace of conscience; for this is only obtainable through the
blood of the Lord Jesus. Having seen *that* blood, God forgives
our sins and remembers them no more. This is characteristic of
the New Covenant. The word of God is quite clear on this
point. If anyone is still bothered by his past sins and has no rest
in his conscience, let him sing the following hymn till he can
respond with an amen in his heart. Then shall he enjoy the
New Covenant blessing of the remission of sins.

> *Why should I worry, doubt and fear?*
> *Has God not caused His Son to bear*
> *My sins upon the tree?*
> *The debt that Christ for me has paid,*
> *Would God another mind have made*
> *To claim again from me?*
>
> *Redemption full the Lord has made,*
> *And all my debts has fully paid,*
> *From law to set me free.*
> *I fear not for the wrath of God,*
> *For I've been sprinkled with His blood,*
> *It wholly covers me.*
>
> *For me forgiveness He has gained,*
> *And full acquittal was obtained,*
> *All debts of sin are paid;*
> *God would not have His claim on two,*
> *First on His Son, my Surety true,*
> *And then upon me laid.*
>
> *So now I have full peace and rest,*
> *My Savior Christ hath done the best*
> *And set me wholly free;*
> *By His all-efficacious blood*
> *I ne'er could be condemned by God,*
> *For He has died for me!*
> — Translated

CONFESSION AND FORGIVENESS

There is no doubt that a man's sins are forgiven once he realizes he is a sinner and believes in the Lord Jesus. But the question remains whether he needs further forgiveness after he has believed in the Lord and received forgiveness. To answer this question let us first mention the following three points:

(1) Upon our being saved we should not continue in sin (Rom. 6.1, 2) and should not sin any more (John 5.14, 8.11).

(2) Believers nonetheless have the possibility of sinning (1 John, 1.8, 10) and of being overtaken in trespasses when tempted (Gal. 6.1, 1 Cor. 10.12). The dissimulations of Peter and Barnabas (Gal. 2.11-13), and the incest of a brother in Corinth (1 Cor. 5.1, 2, 5, 11 — where the consequence of such sin is most terrible because of the destruction of the flesh on the one hand and the excommunication from the church on the other) are all facts.

(3) However, "whosoever is begotten of God doeth no sin, because his seed abideth in him: and he cannot sin, because he is begotten of God" (1 John 3.9). This refers to the *habit* and *nature* of the regenerated person.

Now that we have clarified these three points, we next want to observe that the more that people have fellowship with God in the light the more they need forgiveness and cleansing. This is clearly taught by the passage in 1 John 1.5-7. Let us see what the Scriptures say about the way to forgiveness.

"If we confess our sins, he is faithful and righteous to forgive us our sins, and to cleanse us from all unrighteousness" (1 John 1.9). A believer who sins must *confess* in order to be forgiven. "If we *confess our sins*" God will forgive us our sins and cleanse us from all unrighteousness because He is faithful and righteous. What is the faithfulness of God? What is the righteousness of God? The first points to His word while the second refers to His action. God's word is faithful and His action is righteous. Since He has said He will forgive us our sins,

He definitely will forgive. Since He has said He will cleanse us from all unrighteousness, He will surely cleanse us from all unrighteousness. In view of the fact that He has sent His Son to die for our sins, He cannot but forgive our sins and cleanse us from all unrighteousness. Therefore, by confessing our sins we lay hold of the covenant He made with us and we ask Him to forgive and to cleanse.

There was once a sister in Swatow whose conscience was restless due to constant accusation. Whenever she met a preacher she would say: "My sins are so great, I do not know if God has forgiven me." One day she met a preacher and made the same statement as usual. Whereupon the preacher read the word in 1 John 1.9 with her and then asked if she had confessed her sins before God. "Indeed, I have confessed and do confess often." "What does God say then?" "God says, if we confess our sins, he is faithful and righteous to forgive us our sins and to cleanse us from all unrighteousness." "What do you say to this?" "I do not know if God has forgiven me."

They read and talked, talked and read, till finally they prayed together. Once more she confessed her sins before God. After prayer, she was again asked: "Has God forgiven your sins yet?" "I do not know," she replied. So the preacher challenged her solemnly, "Do you think God has lied?" "How dare I?" "Then what does God say He does 'if we confess our sins'? Has He not said that 'he is faithful and righteous to forgive us our sins and to cleanse us from all unrighteousness'? And at that instant she began to understand, and her conscience entered into rest. Thereafter, until the day she slept in the Lord, she was full of joy. The word of the Lord enlightened and comforted her.

In view of this, we ought to remember that forgiveness is a matter of covenant. If we confess our sins according to God's word, God will also according to His covenant forgive us. Let me therefore ask, Do you dare to lay hold of God's word and pray, "Oh God, You have said if we confess our sins You will forgive us and cleanse us"? We should understand that the reason God makes covenant with us is for us to speak to Him according to the covenant. He wants us to ask Him in faith. We are asking Him to fulfill His word of the covenant, not begging Him for mercy. We are claiming as our portion what is defined in the covenant. Thank God, forgiveness is a part of the New Covenant.

Some may presume that if they could abhor sin more deeply or sorrow for sin more persistently, they would more easily be forgiven. Such a presumption is erroneous because it is not supported by the word of God. Abhorrence and sorrow for sin are the natural results of enlightenment, not conditions to be met in exchange for forgiveness. There is a story in "The Secret of a Happy Christian's Life" which in gist is as follows: A sister once asked a girl, "What will you do if you sin? How will the Lord Jesus treat you?" Her answer was: "I will confess my sin to the Lord, and after He makes me suffer for a while He will forgive me."

Do not think this is only the word of a child, for many grown-ups have the same story. Many people are doing exactly this very thing. They think that after confession there needs to be a period of suffering before they are forgiven. They wait until their hearts ache no more—and this they take to be the assurance of forgiveness. All who think and do in such manner do not know the characteristic of the New Covenant.

Let it be carefully understood that forgiveness is in the New Covenant. For the sake of the shed blood of the Lord Jesus, God cannot but forgive our sins and cleanse us from all unrighteousness. The moment we accept the Lord, God will forgive us according to what the covenant stipulates. Whenever we confess our sins He will forgive, just as His covenant says. For He is bound by the covenant which He himself has made with us. If we only ask Him according to the word of the covenant, God shall not fail to perform it.

Of course we want to remind everyone that the confession

in view here is the result of seeing sin in the light of God. God's light spares not a single sin. If a person sees sin under His enlightenment, condemns sin as sin, and confesses it before God, he will receive forgiveness and cleansing. God forbid that any should take forgiveness as a talisman and proceed to lie or lose one's temper daily under the precious blood. If so, then such a person treats confession merely as a formula, as a technique. To sin on the one hand and to confess as a routine on the other is not reckoned as confessing in the light of God. This kind of routine confession should be carefully avoided. What we say is that people who have fellowship with God and walk in the light of life see sin more readily; therefore, they need much more of God's forgiveness and the cleansing of the blood. This is the kind of confession that really counts. And with such confession as this there comes the rest of New Covenant forgiveness.

"A rainbow round about the throne" (Rev. 4.3b). What is the sign of a rainbow? It is a token of God's covenant with Noah. The rainbow round about the throne indicates that God has never forgotten His covenant. It also attests to the fact that He will not fail to hear any prayer offered up according to the covenant. As long as the rainbow surrounds the throne He will hear the prayer in the covenant. Amazing grace it surely is that God should give us such surety so as to enable us to pray according to covenant.

Is there anyone who has yet to solve the problem of his sins today? Let him lay them before God, take hold of His word, and believe Him according to His covenant. That one may then rest in His covenant. Many spiritual blessings we have missed because we do not know that God has covenanted with us. Our God has made a covenant with us. His intention is to encourage us to speak to Him according to this covenant that He may in turn perform accordingly.

7 | The Characteristics of the New Covenant: (2) Life and Power

We have already seen how the forgiveness of the New Covenant is a gospel of grace. If anyone believes in this forgiving grace, his conscience will come into rest. We know many of the Lord's people have accepted this forgiving grace. They have not only believed but also testified concerning the forgiveness of their sins and the cleansing of all their unrighteousness. But aside from this part (the forgiveness of sins) the New Covenant includes two other most glorious and precious elements; namely, life and power, and an inward knowledge. These two aspects are largely overlooked, unappreciated and unbelieved by many people. It is one of the main reasons many children of God are so poor and weak spiritually.

Now it is good to have our sins forgiven by God; nevertheless, if we, after being forgiven, remain the same—neither allowing God to obtain what He wants in us nor knowing and doing God's will—then what difference is there between us and the people of Israel who in former days wandered in the wilderness? Where will be the glory of the New Covenant?

We must therefore see the excellencies of the New Covenant. In the days of the Old Covenant God took the Israelites by the hand to lead them forth out of the land of Egypt (Heb. 8.9); in the New Covenant He draws our hearts away from Egypt—that is to say, from the world. In the Old Covenant God put His laws before them; in the New Covenant He puts them into our minds and writes them on our hearts. Under the

Old Covenant, although they were outwardly instructed by men and saw the works of God for forty years, they yet erred in their heart and did not know God's ways. Under the New Covenant we shall not need any outward instruction, because from the least to the greatest of us, all shall know the Lord inwardly.

Let us first see how God puts His laws into our mind and writes them on our heart. Why is this a most glorious and precious part of the New Covenant? Let us read some related Scripture passages:

"This is the covenant that I will make with the house of Israel after those days, saith the Lord; I will put my laws into their mind, and on their heart also will I write them: and I will be to them a God, and they shall be to me a people" (Heb. 8.10). "This is the covenant that I will make with them after those days, saith the Lord: I will put my laws on their heart, and upon their mind also will I write them" (Heb. 10.16).

Both passages mention "put" first and then "write"; but note that in Chapter 8 it is first "into their mind" and then "on their heart" while in Chapter 10 the order is reversed. They speak practically of the same thing.

Both these verses in Hebrews quote from Jeremiah 31.33 which reads: "This is the covenant that I will make with the house of Israel after those days, saith Jehovah: I will put my law in their inward parts, and in their heart will I write it; and I will be their God, and they shall be my people."

Moreover, Ezekiel 36.25-28 speaks of the same thing as is found in Jeremiah 31.31-34; except that some words are clearer in Ezekiel while some are clearer in Jeremiah. Let us now read this passage in Ezekiel: "I will sprinkle clean water upon you, and ye shall be clean: from all your filthiness, and from all your idols, will I cleanse you. A new heart also will I give you, and a new spirit will I put within you; and I will take away the stony heart out of your flesh, and I will give you a heart of flesh. And I will put my Spirit within you, and cause you to walk in my statutes, and ye shall keep mine ordinances, and do them. . . . And ye shall be my people, and I will be your God." These verses touch upon at least five things: (1) cleanse us with clean water, (2) give us a new heart, (3) give us a new spirit, (4) take away the stony heart and give us a heart of flesh, and (5) put His Spirit within us. The combined result of these five matters is: to "cause you to walk in my statutes, and ye shall keep mine ordinances, and do them. . . . And ye shall be my people, and I will be your God."

REGENERATION

In order to understand how God puts His laws in us and writes them on our hearts, it is necessary for us to begin with regeneration. For in regeneration the Holy Spirit puts God's uncreated life into our human spirit. Regeneration is a new thing which happens in the human spirit. It is not a matter of behavior, but a matter of life.

The Creation of Man

To know what regeneration is, we must again go back to the story of the creation of man. "Jehovah God formed man of the dust of the ground, and breathed into his nostrils the breath of life; and man became a living soul" (Gen. 2.7). The "breath of life" here refers to the Spirit—the source of life; for the Lord says elsewhere that "it is the spirit that giveth life" (John 6.63a). This is further confirmed in Job: "The breath of the Almighty giveth me life" (33.4b). The Hebrew for the word "life" in "breath of life" is *chay* and is in the plural. God so breathed that there was produced a twofold life: the spiritual and the soulical. When the inbreathing of God entered man's body it became the spirit of man; but when the human spirit reacted with the body the soul was produced. This explains the origin of our spiritual and soulical lives. It also clearly shows us that man is tripartite: being spirit, soul, and body. The New Testament also divides man into three parts: "May your spirit and soul and body be preserved entire" (1 Thess. 5.23b); "even to the dividing of soul and spirit, of both joints and marrow. . . ." (Heb. 4.12b).

The body is the site of "world-consciousness"; the soul, of "self-consciousness"; and the spirit, of "God-consciousness." With its five senses the body gives man various kinds of sensations. Through this physical body man is able to communicate with the outside world. Consequently, it is the place of "world-consciousness." The soul is comprised of the mind, emotion, will, and so forth; all of these belong to the man himself, being expressions of his personality. Hence it is the place of "self-consciousness." The spirit has the functions of conscience, intuition, and communion; and by these man comes to know his relationship with God and learns to worship and serve Him. It is therefore the place of "God-consciousness."

The spirit controls the whole being through the soul. If the spirit desires to act, it communicates its intention to the soul, which in turn will move the body to obey the command of the spirit. According to God's ordering, the spirit, being the highest part of man, should control the whole being. Nevertheless, the will, being the mainstay of personality, belongs to the soul. This will of man's soul has a sovereign right to choose the rule of the spirit, the rule of the body, or even the rule of self. In view of such power belonging to the soul—which is also the seat of personality—the Bible calls man "a living soul."

God's Purpose in Creating Man

We have repeatedly emphasized that the eternal purpose of God is to give himself to man. He takes pleasure in entering into man and uniting with him so that man may have His life and His nature. After God had created Adam He put him in the garden of Eden. In the midst of the garden were the tree of life and the tree of the knowledge of good and evil (Gen. 2.9). These two trees were most conspicuous, they could easily attract man's attention. God gave command to man, saying, "Of every tree of the garden thou mayest freely eat: but of the tree of the knowledge of good and evil, thou shalt not eat of it: for in the day that thou eatest thereof thou shalt surely die" (Gen. 2.16-17). Turning it around, this statement meant that the fruit of the tree of life could be eaten. Had man eaten the fruit of the tree of life he would have chosen God, because the tree of life pointed to God. Oh how grand and beautiful is the purpose of the Creator towards man!

Just as man was created by God, so his original life was also given by God. Speaking of man's originally created life, the Bible indicates that it was upright (Eccles. 7.29) and "very good" (Gen. 1.31). But so far as God's eternal purpose was concerned, man did not yet have God's own uncreated life. Hence he must needs choose God and God's life. [Three different words are used in Greek for "life": (1) *Bios*—this points to the fleshly life. The Lord Jesus used this word when He said of the poor widow that she had cast in all the *living* that she had (Luke 21.4). (2) *Psuche*—this points to man's animated life, the natural life of man—which is the soul life. Whenever the Bible mentions man's life as such, this word is used (Matt. 16.26, Luke 9.24). (3) *Zoe*—this points to the highest life, the spirit life, God's uncreated life. The Bible uses this word when it speaks of "eternal life" (John 3.16).]

The Fall of Man

Mankind has fallen and sinned. This occurred when the man Adam rejected life and ate the forbidden fruit of the tree of the knowledge of good and evil. Formerly man's spirit was open to communicate with God, but now it is alienated from God (Eph. 4.18) and is dead to Him through transgressions (Col. 2.13, Eph. 2.1). At the very beginning God had forewarned Adam, saying, "In the day that thou eatest thereof thou shalt surely die" (Gen. 2.17). So far as Adam's physical body was concerned, he lived for several hundred more years after he had eaten the fruit of the tree of the knowledge of good and evil (Gen. 5.3–5). Consequently, the death here could not have meant the death of the body alone; the spirit in man must have died first.

Death is defined as alienation from life. God is the God of life. In being alienated from Him, Adam was alienated from life. By our saying that Adam's spirit had died we do not mean to suggest that he no longer had a spirit, but that this merely signifies that his spirit had lost its communication with God, having lost its spiritual sensibility. Adam's spirit—though it still existed—was dead towards God. Adam lost the basic ability of the spirit. For as soon as man falls into sin he becomes carnal (Rom. 7.14) and is controlled by his soul. He cannot know the things of God (1 Cor. 2.14); neither is he subject to the law of God, nor indeed can he be, because whoever is in the flesh cannot please God (Rom. 8.7,8).

Will God's eternal purpose fail to be obtained? Not at all; for God is still God, unless He has no will or purpose. But if He *has* an excellent will and eternal plan, God will surely carry it out. He will yet give His own life to man by entering into man and uniting with him in life. But how will it be done? He will come to solve the sin problem, rescue the fallen man, release His life through His Son, and regenerate man by the Holy Spirit.

The Salvation of God

In order to solve the problem of sin and to rescue fallen man, God sent Christ to the world. On the cross Christ bore our sins in His body, "that we, having died unto sins, might live unto righteousness" (1 Peter 2.24). This is typified in the Old Testament period by Moses lifting up the serpent in the wilderness (Num. 21.4-9). Because of their sin the people of Israel deserved death; but God commanded Moses to lift up the brazen serpent in the wilderness so that all who were bitten by the serpent might look and live. In like manner, Christ was lifted up to bear our sins and to die for us that all who were dead in transgressions might receive God's life and live (John 3.14,15).

God would have His life released, and so He put His life in Christ (John 1.4, 1 John 5.11). Christ died on the cross in order to release God's life that was hidden in Him. For Christ was that grain of wheat which fell into the ground and died to release the life of God (John 12.24). Hence by the resurrection of Jesus Christ from the dead God regenerates us (1 Peter 1.3).

Regeneration is being born "of God" (John 1.13), born "of heaven" (1 Cor. 15.47).

Regeneration is being "born of water and the Spirit" (John 3.5). This needs a little explanation. When John the Baptist came to preach and to baptize he proclaimed: "I baptized you in water; but he shall baptize you in the Holy Spirit" (Mark 1.8). Just as in Mark 1 John the Baptist joined the water and the Holy Spirit together, so in John 3 our Lord Jesus also joined the water and the Holy Spirit. Now since the water which John referred to was the water of baptism, then the water which the Lord Jesus spoke of must also be the water of baptism. The word the Lord answered Nicodemus with must be something which the latter could quickly grasp. At that time many people knew of John baptizing with water. It was but natural for Nicodemus to take the water which the Lord Jesus mentioned as being the baptism of John. Had the Lord had another thought in mind concerning water, it would not have been easily comprehended by Nicodemus. We may therefore conclude that "water" here points to the water of baptism.

The baptism of John was "the baptism of repentance, saying unto the people that they *should believe on him that should come after him,* that is, on *Jesus*" (Acts 19.4). The baptism of repentance in which John baptized with water could not regenerate people. Except one be born "of water and the Spirit" he is not born again. The baptism of repentance announces that not only man's behavior—being deadly wicked—needs to be repented of, but also man himself—being corrupted and dead—must be buried in baptism. When one enters the water to be baptized he is confessing before God how wicked is his behavior and how corrupted and dead in transgressions he is, that he deserves nothing but death and burial.

Yet man is not born again "of water" alone; he must be born both "of water *and* the Spirit." He must receive the gift of the Holy Spirit from the Lord Jesus before he can have God's life. John the Baptist preached "repentance" first (Mark 1.4), with the Lord Jesus following immediately by adding "believe" to it (Mark 1.15). Repentance delivers us from all which belongs to us. Believing gets us into all which belongs to God. We enter the water through repentance, we receive the Holy Spirit by faith. To enter the water and to receive the Holy Spirit in this way is to be born "of water and the Spirit." To repent and enter the water concludes the life of the old man; to believe and be joined to the Holy Spirit is to receive the life of God. This is regeneration.

Although regeneration is being born of water and the Holy Spirit, the work of regeneration in its subjective aspect is all done by the Holy Spirit (the objective aspect of the work of regeneration is all done by Christ). It is for this reason that the Lord Jesus in John 3 mentioned "born of water" once but "born of the Spirit" three times (vv.5,6,8).

Regeneration is being "born of the Spirit." The Holy Spirit comes to induce people to repent. He "will convict the world in respect of sin" (John 16.8). He guides people to accept by faith the Lord Jesus as Savior; He enters those who have thus repented and believed and gives them God's life, so regenerating them. The Holy Spirit enlightens people to bring them to repentance; the Holy Spirit guides people to believe that they may receive the life of God. All this is recorded in the Scriptures as gospel truth. And hence the Bible tells us that God begets us with the gospel which is also the word of truth (1 Cor. 4.15, James 1.18). We are "begotten again, not of corruptible seed, but of incorruptible, through the word of God, which liveth and abideth" (1 Peter 1.23). Through the Holy Spirit God uses His word to impart His life to us and have it planted in us. We are moved by the Holy Spirit into believing God's word and thus receiving God's life. In God's word the life of God is hidden; indeed, His words "are life" (John 6.63). As soon as we accept God's word we receive His life.

The life which we obtain in regeneration is not carnal but spiritual. It is like the wind, invisible yet sensible, and it is most practical (John 3.8). Regeneration, therefore, is none other than having, besides man's own life, the life of God.

As soon as we are regenerated we receive "the right to become children of God" (John 1.12); and this commences a father-and-son relationship with God in life (Gal. 4.6, Rom. 8.15,16). God's uncreated life—that which is "eternal life" (John 17.3) and which Adam failed to receive and which we did not have—now comes into us. This is the character and the glory of the New Covenant. Hallelujah!

God's life has a nature of its own; so we who have His life are made "partakers of the divine nature" (2 Peter 1.4). It is now possible for us to know God's will, to love to do His pleasure, and to live out the image of God (Col. 3.10). Should a person profess to have received the life of God's Son and yet there be not the slightest indication of this new life nature in his daily walk—neither in his loving righteousness nor in hating sin—this man's faith and regeneration is highly questionable. For God's life has its special nature. If a person does not exhibit that nature, how dare he profess to have God's life?

"The spirit of man is the lamp of Jehovah," says Proverbs

20.27. After Adam's fall this spirit had been darkened. But when the Holy Spirit begets us again and puts God's life in us, He quickens our spirit (Eph. 2.5) as though lighting a lamp. In the death of man that was caused by original sin, man's spirit died first. Even so, in regeneration—when the Holy Spirit implants God's uncreated life in man's spirit—the divine Spirit makes alive man's spirit first. The work of the Holy Spirit begins from the inside of man. He works from the center to the circumference, from the spirit to the soul and then to the body. The regenerating work of the Holy Spirit is done purely in the spirit. Formerly our spirit was dead in transgressions, now it is made alive (Col. 2.13). Now it knows God and is sensitive to sin. And for this reason, anyone who says he has been born again and yet neither knows God nor is sensitive to sin brings his experience into question.

When the Holy Spirit begets us He also gives us a "new heart" and puts in us a "new spirit" (Ezek. 36.26). In giving us a new heart God has not given another heart but has simply renewed that corrupted heart of ours. Likewise, in giving us a new spirit God does not give another spirit, He simply makes alive and renews that dead spirit of ours. With a new heart we may now think of God, desire after Him, and love Him. With this new heart we develop a new delight and inclination towards heavenly and spiritual things. And with a new spirit we will not be feeble towards spiritual matters nor dull towards the things of God as we were once before. Instead, with the new spirit we will be strong in spiritual things and be discerning in the things of God (1 Cor. 2.12). We will be able to commune with God.

Another glorious fact is, that when we are born again God also puts His Spirit in us (Ezek. 36.27). The Holy Spirit now dwells in our renewed spirit. This never happened in the dispensation of the Old Covenant. True, during the time of the Old Testament the Holy Spirit worked upon man, but the Bible never distinctly records that in those days the Holy Spirit dwelt forever in man.

How do we know that in the dispensation of the New Covenant the Holy Spirit dwells forever in us? This is plainly indicated to the disciples by our Lord himself: "I will pray the Father, and he shall give you another Comforter, that he may be with you *for ever,* even the Spirit of truth: whom the world cannot receive; for it beholdeth him not, neither knoweth him: ye know him; for he abideth with you, and shall be *in* you" (John 14.16-17). The coming of this Comforter is but the Lord coming in another form, because He continues by saying: "I will not leave you desolate: I come unto you" (v.18). The "he" in verse 17 is the "I" here in verse 18. Hence this "another Comforter" is but the Lord coming himself in a different form.

When the Lord was on earth He was often with the disciples, yet He could not abide in them. Since His resurrection, though, He has been clothed with the Holy Spirit and can consequently dwell in them. As God comes among men in and through Christ, so Christ comes into men in and through the Holy Spirit. The Holy Spirit in us is the same as Christ in us (Rom. 8.9, 2 Cor. 13.5). Christ in us is the same as God in us (the "Christ" in Ephesians 3.17 is the "God" in Ephesians 3.19). Oh, how blessed this is—that the Creator indwells the created! This is the most marvelous, blessed, and glorious thing in the universe.

The Lord will not leave us as orphans. He will himself take care of us, nourishing us, edifying us, and bearing the full responsibility for us. In other words, the indwelling Holy Spirit is to translate into our subjective experience the objective fact of what Christ has accomplished for us on the cross. The Spirit of truth is to guide us into the reality. ("Comforter" in the Greek original includes two thoughts: one means "called to one's side"—that is, to one's aid. This is to say that the Holy Spirit is our present help. Whenever we need His aid, He is always alongside us to help. The other means "one who pleads another's cause" — an advocate. Christ, as it were, appears before God to plead for us — that is, to plead for our good).

The moment we are regenerated, we become saved people. For God "saved us, through the washing of regeneration" (Titus 3.5). Regeneration not only gives us life, it in addition washes away our old creation; for it is also a "washing." It delivers us from the old creation.

We were formerly an old creation; but now "through . . . the renewing of the Holy Spirit" (Titus 3.5) we have received a new heart, a new spirit, and an uncreated life. "Wherefore if any man is in Christ, there is a new creation: the old things are passed away; behold, they are become new" (2 Cor. 5.17 mg.).

Once a person possesses God's life he is capable of knowing God and things spiritual. Spiritually he is today in the kingdom of God; prophetically he will enter the kingdom of God in the future (John 3.3,5).

With regeneration he has not only come into possession of God's life today but is also begotten "unto a living hope . . ., unto an inheritance incorruptible, and undefiled, and that fadeth not away, reserved in heaven" (1 Peter 1.3-4). Today he becomes a heavenly man on earth, later he will enjoy the heavenly portion reserved for him in heaven.

Praise and thank God, for how marvelous is regeneration, how blessed and glorious is the fruit of regeneration!

Having been regenerated, we now belong to the godly race. But we still must grow to maturity, that is, we must grow to be like the God-Man who is in glory. We know each kind of life has its own characteristic and instinct. For instance, a bird with a bird's life has its own life characteristic and instinct. It loves to fly in the air, and it possesses the ability to fly. A fish with a fish's life has its own life characteristic and instinct too. It enjoys living in the water and possesses the capability of doing so. This is not only true of animal life; it works the same way with plant life. "Even so every good tree bringeth forth good fruit; but the corrupt tree bringeth forth evil fruit. A good tree cannot bring forth evil fruit, neither can a corrupt tree bring forth good fruit" (Matt. 7.17-18). This is the natural law of life. To us who are born again and have the life of God, this new life naturally has its own characteristic and instinct too.

We need to understand, however, that although the life we receive is perfect, it is not matured. The life itself is so perfect that it has the potential of arriving at the highest level, yet at the time of regeneration it is so newly born that it awaits to grow into maturity. Like a newborn plant, its life is perfect and yet it is raw. The perfection of the newly born is limited to the life source, but the perfection of maturity applies to every area of the organism. This explains why a man who is regenerated needs to be renewed continuously by the Holy Spirit so that this new life may be perfected in every part of his being. In the following pages we will try to show how this seed of life manifests its own characteristic and instinct.

THE LAW OF LIFE

Let us again read Hebrews 8.10: "I will put my laws into their mind, and on their heart also will I write them." Here lies the difference between the New Covenant and the Old. In the Old Covenant the law was placed outside of men, having been written on tables of stone; in the New Covenant it is put into our mind and written on our heart. What is outside and written on tables of stone must be of the letter (2 Cor. 3.6). What, then, is the law which can be put within us and written on our heart? What is the nature of this law? From the word of God we find that the law which can be put into our mind and written on our heart is not of the letter but of life. Each law may not be of life, but every life has its law. The law which God puts in us is the life which He gives to us.

As soon as anyone has God's life, he has this law of life within him. God comes among men in His Son, and God's Son comes into men in the Holy Spirit. It is the Holy Spirit who brings to us this life, and the operation of this life in us is what is here called the law of life. In other words, this law of life comes from the Holy Spirit. This is what Romans 8.2 defines as "the law of the Spirit of life." And this law is singular in number. The law in the Old Covenant contains many articles, whereas the law in the New Covenant does not have articles one, two, three, on up to the last one; for it has but one article, which is the law of life. This is the New Covenant.

What is the nature of this law of life? Such a nature will operate spontaneously along a certain line. For instance, the ear will spontaneously hear and the eye will instinctively see without the need of it being forcibly controlled. So too will the tongue taste food, swallowing naturally what is good and spitting out what is bad—all without the need of any conscious effort. Were the ear not to hear, the eye not to see, and the tongue not to distinguish the taste, that person must be either physically ill or lifeless. What God puts in us is life, and this life is a law by itself. He has not placed in us a mere outward form or letter; He instead puts in us a living law of life which operates spontaneously.

Let us illustrate this as follows: Suppose you speak to a dead peach tree, saying, "You should have green leaves and red flowers, and at the appointed time bear peaches." You can say this from the beginning of the year to the end and yet get nothing, because it is dead. If it is a live peach tree, though, it will quite naturally sprout, leaf, blossom, and yield fruit without your asking at all. This is called the law of life, for it operates automatically.

Since what God has put in us is life, it naturally is a law, which operates spontaneously. This law will automatically "law" out life. And this life will spontaneously "law" out the contents of the life within us—even "law" out the riches of God. It will naturally flow if it is not obstructed.

LAWS AND THE INWARD PARTS

"I will put my law in their inward parts, and in their heart will I write it" (Jer. 31.33b). To what do these inward parts refer? In order to understand we have to mention this matter of the "heart" (by heart here we do not mean the physiological organ). We will delve into this "heart" matter according to the record of the Scriptures and the experiences of many of the Lord's people. So far as the Bible record is concerned, the heart seems to embrace the following parts:

(1) Conscience is attached to the heart—"having our hearts sprinkled from an evil conscience" (Heb. 10.22); "if our heart condemn us" (1 John 3.20). Condemning is a function of conscience, showing then that conscience is within the realm of the heart.

(2) Mind too is linked to the heart—"Jesus knowing their thoughts said, Wherefore think ye evil in your hearts?" (Matt. 9.4); "reasoning in their hearts" (Mark 2.6); "the imagination of their heart" (Luke 1.51); "wherefore do questionings arise in your heart?" (Luke 24.38). All these instances are stories about the heart. "And understand with their heart" (Matt. 13.15); "pondering them in her heart" (Luke 2.19); "quick to discern the thoughts . . . of the heart" (Heb. 4.12). All these verses indicate that the mind is linked to the heart.

(3) Will is also tied to the heart—"with purpose of heart they would cleave unto the Lord" (Acts 11.23); "ye became obedient from the heart" (Rom. 6.17); "purposed in his heart" (2 Cor. 9.7); "intents of the heart" (Heb. 4.12). These all reveal that will is definitely linked to the heart.

(4) And emotion is joined to the heart—"his heart fainted"

(Gen. 45.26); "Was not our heart burning within us?" (Luke 24.32); "Let not your heart be troubled" (John 14.27). All of these passages confirm that emotion is joined to the heart.

On the basis of the above passages—and though we dare not assert that conscience is the heart, that mind is the heart, or that will is the heart, or emotion is the heart—we dare to affirm that the heart has at least conscience, mind, will, and emotion attached to it. The heart is able to exercise control over conscience, mind, will, and emotion. It may be said that the heart is the sum total of these four things. Conscience is the conscience of the heart; mind, the mind of the heart; will, the will of the heart; and emotion, the emotion of the heart.

Hence the "inward parts" of Jeremiah 31.33 include at least conscience, mind, will, and emotion of the heart.

The Relation between Heart and Laws

What does it mean by "laws" in both Hebrews 8.10 and 10.16? We have mentioned before that the law of life is singular, not plural, in number. Why then do we find "laws" in these places? Why is "laws" plural in number? It can be explained in the following way. The life which we receive at regeneration is a law. This refers to the law itself. But the operation of this law in us is more than one. God's life has its operation in all our inward parts. It operates in our spirit, in our mind, in our will, in our emotion. So that what Jeremiah records—"I will put my law in their *inward parts*"—points to the operation of the law of God's life in every inward segment of man.

So far as the law itself is concerned, it is singular; but as far as the operation of this law goes, it is plural. It can be likened to the water we use. The source is one, yet the pipes are many. The life in us is one law, though it operates in all our inward parts. The life is one, while its operations are many. It works in all the inward parts, nonetheless its source is but one.

Heart Is the Passage of Life

Even though the spirit is the highest part of man, what really represents him is not his spirit but his heart. "Commune with your own heart" (Ps. 4.4) coincides with what is commonly understood to be "heart and mouth consulting together."* We may say that the heart is the real "I"; without question it is the most important thing in our daily living.

The heart stands between the spirit and the soul. All that enters the spirit must pass through the heart; so also is it true with all that issues from the spirit. "Keep thy heart with all diligence; for out of it are the issues of life" (Prov. 4.23). This means that the heart is the passage of life. In other words, all fruits which man bears outwardly come from the heart. Such is its significance.

The heart is the passage or channel through which life must operate. It is for this reason that God must first move upon our heart before His life can enter into us. Had there been no sorrow of heart or repentance, God's life would not be able to come in. God has to touch our heart—causing us either to sense the pain of sin or to taste the sweetness of His love and the preciousness of Christ—in order to bring us to repentance. Heartache is a matter of the conscience, while repentance is a change of mind. When our heart is so touched, our volition will decide and our heart will believe. And thus will the life of God enter into us as is a seed that is planted in us (1 Peter 1.23).

The Heart Is the Switch of Life

A living seed that is sown in the ground is able to grow and grow, but its growth is not without condition. If, for example, a seed is never watered after it is sown, its growth will be hin-

---

*A Chinese proverb. — *Translator*

dered. This is not only true with plant life; it works the same with physical things. For instance, the power of electricity is enormous, yet if a tiny switch is off, it can stop the current. The power of spiritual life is indeed great and spontaneous, but its growth will be limited if the conditions for growth are not met.

How, then, can this life be expanded? We should not forget that just as the acceptance of life commences from the heart so the growth of life must also start from the heart. Whether our spiritual life expands or not depends on how open our heart is towards God. If our heart is open to Him our life will expand; but if our heart is closed, it has no possibility of expansion. So, then, it comes back to the matter of the heart. We cannot afford to overlook this.

We ought to recognize that the heart has its delight and inclination. To worship and serve God is not a matter of the heart, rather is it a matter of the spirit. On the other hand, to desire after God and to love Him is not a matter of the spirit but is of the heart. The heart can love God but it cannot touch Him. It may incline towards God but it cannot commune with Him. That which may touch God and communicate with Him is the spirit.

Some people are of the opinion that we should use our brain in touching the things of God just as we need to use our brain in hearing sounds. True, the hearing of sounds does require the use of the brain, yet it also requires the use of the ear. If a person is talking and you have no ear, can you understand the meaning of such sounds? The eye is to see things with and to distinguish colors such as red, white, yellow, and blue. Suppose you have no eye; can you distinguish the colors? If you desire to see, you have to use the eyes. Sounds will be transmitted to the brain through ears; even so, spiritual things must be touched by the spirit.

Nevertheless, should you be a heartless person God is still

unable to commune and communicate with you. Your heart is like the switch of an electric lamp. If the switch is on, the light shines; if it is off, the light disappears. If your heart is open to God it is easy for Him to commune and communicate with you. But if your heart is closed to Him it will be difficult for God to commune and communicate with you. God's life in us is a fact, nonetheless the heart is the switch of that life. Whether His life can flow from our spirit to our conscience, mind, will or emotion depends on the heart that serves as a switch. With an opened heart His life will reach all our inward parts; with a closed one, His life will not be able to get through.

The Heart May Block Life's Operation

After we are regenerated by the Holy Spirit we possess an uncreated life, even the life of God. This life is full of power, a power which is infinite and unrestricted by time and space. Yet if our heart is a problem, God's life will be seriously blocked. Should there be any problem in our conscience the life of God will doubtless be hindered. Should there be a problem in our mind or emotion or our will, again, God's life will be obstructed. Yes, God's life is placed within our spirit, but it needs to flow into all our inward parts. It will be blocked if any of our inward parts presents a problem.

It is a matter of fact that each one who by grace belongs to the Lord has God's life in him. This is positive and undeniable. That this life of God in us is both alive and operative is also positive and undeniable: and having God's life in us, we should experience revelation, enlightenment, an inner voice, and an inner sensation. Even so, many of God's children are asking why they do not have revelation, enlightenment, inner voice and sensation. Is it because God's life is not actually in them? Or that God's life is not living in them? The answer is of course no. It is positive and undeniable that God's life is in us and is both alive and operative. We do not have revelation, en-lightenment, inner voice, and inner sensation because on our side the "heart" causes problems. Either our conscience be-comes a problem due to our not dealing with what it con-demns, or our mind is bewildered by cares, evil thoughts, argu-ments or doubts. If it is not a problem of the will such as our being headstrong or disobedient, it may be a problem of the emotion such as carnal desire or some natural inclination. A part of the heart must have become a problem or hindrance.

The life of God is put in us, and this life will issue forth from our spirit. Yet sometimes we do not allow it to pass through. Due to an obstacle raised by our conscience, mind, will or emotion, God's life is unable to "law" out from us. Let us always keep in mind that in expanding outwardly, the life of God must pass through the various parts of the heart. Any problem in any segment of the heart will block its operation.

We may prove this by the words in Ephesians 4.17–19. "This I say therefore, and testify in the Lord, that ye no longer walk as the Gentiles also walk, in the vanity of their mind [original: *nous*], being darkened in their understanding [original: *dianoia*], alienated from the life of God, because of the ignorance that is in them, because of the hardening of their heart; who being past feeling gave themselves up to lasciviousness, to work all uncleanness with greediness."

[Note: the word *nous* in verse 17 is used over twenty times in the New Testament. *Nous*—that is, mind—denotes, speak-ing generally, the seat of reflective consciousness, comprising the faculties of perception and understanding, as well as those of feeling, judging and determining. Its use may be analyzed as follows. It denotes (a) the faculty of knowing, the seat of the un-derstanding: Luke 24.45, Rom. 1.28 and 14.5, 1 Cor. 14.15,19, Eph. 4.17, Phil. 4.7, Col. 2.18, 1 Tim. 6.5, 2 Tim 3.8, Titus 1.15, and Rev. 13.18 and 17.9; (b) counsels, purpose: Rom. 11.34—i.e., the purpose of the mind of God, 12.2, 1 Cor. 1.10

and 2.16—twice used in 2.16 to indicate first the thoughts and counsels of God and second the thoughts and counsels of Christ which is a testimony to His Godhood—and Eph. 4.23; (c) the new nature, which belongs to the believer by reason of the new birth: Rom. 7.23,25—where it is contrasted with the flesh as the principle of evil which dominates fallen man.*

[*Nous* includes in its meaning both understanding and thought. Though we dare not say the *nous* is all that the mind is, it is undoubtedly the main part of the mind nevertheless. And it is for this reason that it is translated "mind" in English. As human beings we have three organs for knowledge: physically, the brain; spiritually, the intuition; and soulically, the *nous*, which is also controlled by the intuition. We all know about the physical brain. And as to intuition, we sometimes sense its presence, sometimes not. At times it constrains us; at other times it restrains us. This something within us is called intuition. *Nous* stands in between intuition and brain. It discloses the meaning of intuition and causes the brain to think through. In case the *nous* is deficient we will be unable to express our inward meaning, even if our intuition is strong and our brain is good. Now the *nous* in verse 17 is the thinking organ—just as the "eye" is a seeing organ; whereas the *dianoia* —understanding—in verse 18 is a function of this thinking organ, just as "seeing" may be considered to be the function of the eye.]

The vanity of the mind (or *nous*), as quoted earlier in the passage from Ephesians 4.17-19, is what we commonly call building castles in the air. It is a vain thought. The mind of

---

*The above paragraph is based almost entirely on W.E. Vine, *An Expository Dictionary of New Testament Words* (Old Tappan, N.J.: Fleming H. Revell Co., 1966), III, p. 69. Since Watchman Nee was found discussing the subject of the *nous* in such great detail here, it was thought helpful to the reader to use Vine's descriptive analysis of the biblical references as the best way of presenting what Mr. Nee had to say in the above paragraph. Mr. Nee's own words resume in the next paragraph below.—*Translator.*

such a person is fully occupied with a kind of vain thought. There was once a story about a man who was asked to pray at the conclusion of the preacher's sermon. As he did so he could not help praying about his fifty-two strings of money (at the time, coins in China were tied to strings). This man's mind was pre-occupied with the vain thought of money. How, then, could the life of God be released when it reached that inward part? Through this example, we can see that a person, thing, or event may each become a kind of vain thought and occupy our mind. Whenever our mind is usurped by any vain thought, God's life is choked (Matt. 13.22).

As soon as man's mind is occupied by vanity, his understanding is darkened and his ability to comprehend turns dull. Once a young Christian was caught up with a certain matter. He pondered upon it until his head grew dizzy. Suddenly he thought it was God's will, but equally as suddenly he concluded it was *not* God's will. His mind turned and churned until he was utterly perplexed. This was due to the darkening of his *dianoia* — his power of comprehension was obscured.

How does the mind become vain, the understanding darkened, and the person alienated from the life of God? It is all because of the ignorance in him, because of the hardening of his heart which casts off all feelings. The heart is hardened to such a degree that it no longer has any feeling. It all originates with the heart.

We may say then that if the heart is hardened the person will become alienated from the life of God. He will grow more ignorant and less able to understand. And the growth of life will consequently be hindered. From this we may conclude that the law of life is at work in us, waiting to "law" out through the inward parts of our being; but its operation will be blocked if there is any problem in the various elements of the heart. In order to allow God's life to expand freely, the heart must be beyond reproach.

Softening of the Stony Heart and
the Question of Life

Ezekiel 36.25–27 speaks of at least five things: (1) cleanse us with clean water, (2) give us a new heart, (3) put within us a new spirit, (4) take away from us the stony heart and give us a heart of flesh, and (5) put within us God's own Spirit. The combined outcome of these five matters causes us to walk in God's statutes and to keep His ordinances and do them.

We have already touched upon the new heart and the new spirit and the Holy Spirit indwelling us. We shall now deal briefly with how God takes away our stony heart and gives us a heart of flesh. It should be understood that in referring to a stony heart and a heart of flesh it does not mean that we have two hearts; for our heart is only one. The stony heart has reference to the hardness of the heart, while the heart of flesh has reference to a softness or tenderness of heart. The heart is still one in number.

At the time we are saved we are given a heart of flesh by God; even so, our stony heart still exists. It may be said that on the one hand we have a heart of flesh and on the other hand a heart of stone. The taking away of the stony heart is not an instantaneous matter; rather, it is softened gradually. The progress of God's life in us depends wholly on the degree of the softening of our heart. As our stony heart is gradually transformed into a heart of flesh, the life of God is progressively able to operate without hindrance.

Concerning this matter the children of God have many similar experiences. On the day a person gets saved his hardened heart is softened, yet we dare not say it is totally softened. It may be at that time that his heart is softened seventy percent. A little while later, however, it begins to become hardened again. His heart seems to revert to its former hardened state. This stiffening of the heart is a gradual process. He may be seized by some affair or affected by some person or entangled by some particular thing or even magnetized by some work. He falls because of these causes; and his heart again becomes the problem.

Hence the progress of our life hinges entirely on the transformation of our heart—whether it is hard or soft. If our heart is seized by anything outside of God—be it an affair, a person, or a thing—the operation of life will as a rule be hindered. For this reason God will transform our heart continuously until it wholly becomes flesh. Then His Spirit is able to cause our inner life to expand with strength.

For God's life to expand out from us He must touch our heart and soften its hardness. Some are touched by the love of God, others are reached by the chastening of God. At one time the children of Israel were so rebellious against God that He had to smite them to bring them back to himself. One sister may be so occupied with her child, being indulgent only towards him, that God may—after repeated warnings—have to take him away in order to restore her heart to God. Or a certain brother may be so engrossed in his business that after warning him ten times without response God has to let his business fail. Only then will his heart return to God. Or one who serves the Lord can be so magnetized by work, burying himself from dawn to dusk in it, that his heart is stolen away from God through His being replaced by work. God speaks once, even ten times, but he will not hear. So God smites him. And when he falls, his heart begins to understand and he turns back to Him.

Some brothers and sisters have their honors and specialties and righteousnesses, yet these honors and specialties and righteousnesses which they strictly guard over become both their boastings and the measurements against which they measure other people. These things have literally choked their hearts. God speaks once, twice, ten times and twenty times, but they will not listen. Finally, His hand must come down on them.

Whereupon they suddenly realize and are prostrated before God. Their hearts once again turn completely to Him.

God so works in order to transform the stony heart into a heart of flesh so that His life can operate without hindrance. If our heart is touched by God we will naturally say to Him, "O God, I consecrate myself to You, I want to turn to You with my whole heart." And the moment we offer ourselves to allow Him to work, He will commence His operation in us. And as He operates, we will see and hear and sense something within. Just be willing to obey God and His life will move into the conscience, mind, will, and emotion of your heart. It will keep on moving.

TWO CONDITIONS FOR LIFE'S OPERATION

The law of life seeks to move out from our spirit that it may operate through our various inward parts. Oftentimes, however, it cannot pass through, as though striking a wall. This is because we have blocked it. In order to let the life operate freely, we must fulfill two conditions.

Obey Life's First Impulse

One of the conditions is that we should obey life's first impulse. It should be noted that the unregenerated has no inward feeling at all; only he who is born again possesses at least something of such an inward feeling.

Once a Christian physician said to a preacher, "Spiritual beginning and spiritual growth come from hunger and thirst. Many people feel neither hungry nor thirsty. How can we help them to feel so?" Replied the preacher, "You are a physician. You know that there is life in man. Unless he is dead he will more or less have the desire for food. How, then, can you increase his desire for food? You give him some medicine to stim-

ulate him until his desire for food becomes normal. In the same
way, the one who has some inward feeling must learn to obey
such an impulse. If you obey this little feeling your hunger and
thirst will increase a little. More obedience results in stronger
hunger and thirst. As your inward feeling grows stronger, you
obey a little more; and as you obey still further, your inward
feeling increases that much more. More obedience means more
inward feeling. Thus you immediately realize you are inwardly
alive."

This is the way life will operate in us. It turns towards the
emotional part of our heart, causing us to move towards God;
next it turns to the mental part of our heart, drawing us to
God; and then it turns to the volitional part, motivating us
towards God even more. By such cycles of turnings, our
spiritual life is increased and deepened and heightened.
Therefore, we need to begin by *obeying the tiniest inward feeling*. As soon as we sense such an impulse, we must learn to
obey.

Some may ask this question: What happens after obedience? To which we would reply: Before a person has obeyed
his first inward feeling he need not be concerned with the
afterwards. According to the Bible God never gives a person
two feelings at the same time. Abraham is a good example.
When he went out, he knew not where he went (Heb. 11.8). He
only knew that God called him to go out from his homeland
and kindred and come into the land which God would show
him (Acts 7.3). His first inward feeling was to get out of Ur of
Chaldea. The guiding life will never cause us to be independent; it always leads us to trusting.

This experience of Abraham affirms the fact that when a
person takes the first step he does not know what the next step
will be. Abraham simply walked step by step, trusting as he
went. God not only gave Abraham faith, He in addition incor-
porated His life and nature into Abraham. Hence after we take
one step in obedience we must look to God and commit our

next step to Him. Thus will He guide us step by step. As by the grace of God we learn to follow Him inwardly and progressively, there will be feelings in our inward being.

One thing very precious is the fact that if we overstep the bounds set by God or if our action does not agree with our inner life, we will immediately sense our being "forbidden of the Holy Spirit" (Acts 16.6) and that "the Spirit of Jesus suffer[s] [us] not" (Acts 16.7). By obeying the inner guidance in our goings and stayings time after time, we shall make progress in life. Let us repeat: we must obey life's first impulse — even the tiniest of feelings — since obedience is an important condition for the operation of life.

Love God

The other condition is to love God: "Thou shalt love the Lord thy God with all thy heart, and with all thy soul, and with all thy mind, and with all thy strength" (Mark 12.30). The word "mind" here is *dianoia* in the Greek. According to God's word, to love God is related to the operation of life. According to the experience of many saints God first sows His life in them, then He stirs the emotion of their heart by love. If we study the Gospel of John we will see that it stresses love as well as faith. It not only states that "he that believeth on the Son hath eternal life" (3.36) but also asserts that "if a man love me, he will keep my word: and my Father will love him, and we will come unto him, and make our abode with him" (14.23). *By faith life is received; through love life is released.* Faith alone will let life in; love alone will let it out.

We must therefore allow this love to reach into our heart, making its way into the emotional, intellectual, and volitional parts of our heart. Let us lift up our heart and say: "My God, I will love You with my soul, I will love You with my understanding, I will love You with my strength." Whoever says this truthfully will soon see that his thought is changed, his speech is changed, his conduct is changed—all within and without him is changed. And why? Because there is the "story of love" within him. Oh, what God expects of us today is that our heart may be touched by Him; that our soul, our understanding, and our strength may all be touched by Him. "But whensoever it [the heart] shall turn to the Lord, the veil is taken away" (2 Cor. 3.16). As the heart turns to the Lord, there shall come enlightenment, inner voice, and inward feeling.

The question before you and me, then, is not what is enlightenment, or voice, or feeling, but where is your heart? If your heart is attached to a person or thing or affair, or even gift or spiritual experience or spiritual work, your inner life will be hindered in its growth and will not be able to flow out because it cannot pass through your heart. Hence you must *give your heart to the Lord!* It should be attached to Him. If your heart is really towards God you will have enlightenment and inner voice and inward feeling. How, then, are you going to know the will of God? It is not by first understanding it in your head, but rather the heart must first turn to God. You should pray: "O God, I only want You and nothing else." Were this true of you, you would easily know God's will.

Romans 12.1-2 proves this. Paul first says, "I beseech you therefore, brethren, by the mercies of God." This is touching the emotion of the heart. Then he says, "Present your bodies a living sacrifice." This is an act of the will. And finally he says, "Be ye transformed by the renewing of your mind, that ye may prove what is the good and acceptable and perfect will of God." This is to understand God's will in the mind. Thus we are shown how the inner life of man is able to reach into the emotion, the will and the mind of his heart. In this way is life expanded and diffused. When our heart is wholly turned to God, He will give us inward feeling, He will guide us and support us, so that we may have strength within to obey Him. So shall both our inward and outward state be changed. If we want our life to grow and to expand we must love the Lord our

God with all our heart, with all our soul, with all our understanding, and with all our strength!

If we allow the life of God to operate in us by obeying it, this will naturally result in growth and expansion. By letting this life work unceasingly within us—even in our conscience, our mind, our will, and our emotion—it will take away all unwanted things and deposit in us the riches which come from God. This process of subtracting a little and adding a little goes on continually in us. The more the subtraction, the more the addition. What is subtracted is Adam, what is added is Christ. What is subtracted is the old, what is added is the new. What is subtracted is the dead, what is added is the living. Undergoing subtraction and addition little by little, our life continues to grow.

When the life of God operates in us there will be two effects: one is the effect of death, the other is the effect of resurrection. The effect of death takes away the sickness, whereas the effect of resurrection restores health. The first element of the Lord's cross is death, its second element is resurrection. We are told in Romans 6 that these two are the strongest and most effective elements of the life of Christ. Now what is the cross? It is this, that when your heart is touched by God you offer yourself into God's hand in order that His life may operate in you. And as it operates, there is an element which puts you to death. This effect of death takes away from you all which is undesired—that which rebels against God, that which is contrary to life, and that which is contradictory to the Holy Spirit. Meanwhile, there is also a living element, which causes you to live. The effect of this life is to enable you to live out all the riches of the Godhead, and so filling you with light, joy and peace.

This is how both the death and life of Christ work in you to deliver you from sin—from all which God hates and condemns—and at the same time to give you freshness, light, joy and peace. As goes the subtracted so comes the added. The life of God will operate and revolve around until little by little something is removed and something is left. As God's life operates, you will both die a little and come alive a little. It operates without ceasing, taking away more of the undesired and leaving behind more of the desired. The more the dead is removed, the more the living is increased. May we follow the operation of God's life, letting it pass through all our inward parts and work without obstacle so that it may always have something to take away and something to add on.

THE POWER OF LIFE'S OPERATION

"If that first covenant had been faultless, then would no place have been sought for a second" (Heb. 8.7). We have before mentioned that the fault of the first covenant lies not in the covenant itself, rather does it point to what the first covenant could not do in men. For it was written on tables of stone and was stipulated article by article. It required people to keep God's law, yet it did not give them the power to keep these laws. But the New Covenant is a better one, because the law is put in people's minds and written on their hearts that they may obey God's will. Furthermore, they do not need to be taught by men for they shall know God inwardly.

Therefore, we declare that the New Covenant is most precious and exceedingly glorious. As we have pointed out earlier, however, since the laws are put in the inward parts of man, God's life will be blocked and will not be able to expand if it cannot pass through any of those inward parts.

Is the New Covenant, then, subject to the same weakness as

that of the first covenant? Not at all. The New Covenant is able to do what the first covenant could not do: "The things which are impossible with men are possible with God" (Luke 18.27). The New Covenant has power, for the operation of this life is exceedingly powerful. It has "the power of an endless [Greek, *indissoluble*] life" (Heb. 7.16). It is the strength of might which raised the Lord Jesus from the dead (Eph. 1.20). It is also the power which works in us exceedingly abundantly above all that we could ask or think (Eph. 3.20). We will now illustrate this point.

Turning the Heart towards God

In 2 Corinthians 3.14-16 we are told how the minds of the children of Israel were hardened so that even until now, at the reading of the Old Covenant, the same veil remains upon their hearts. But it also tells us that whensoever their hearts ever do turn to the Lord, the veil is taken away. Hence the veil is their hardened heart towards the Lord. Whenever anyone's heart becomes a problem, he too will have a veil within him.

How, then, will our heart turn towards the Lord? The Bible declares that "the king's heart is in the hand of Jehovah as the watercourses: he turneth it whithersoever he will" (Prov. 21.1). If only we are willing to put our heart in God's hand, He is able to turn us around. Should we pray in this manner—"Incline my heart unto thy testimonies, and not to covetousness" (Ps. 119.36)—God will bring about the turning of the heart.

You being a truly saved person, your heart has been renewed. Even if you should ever become cold and turn aside, you know inwardly what has transpired. God has mercy upon you, and His life operates in you, until one day you pray audibly or silently: "O God, incline my heart towards You!" Given this little ground His life operates further, even intensifies, until your heart rises up and turns to God.

Causing Man to Obey God

"Even as ye have always *obeyed* . . . but now *much more*" (Phil. 2.12). How can they obey to such a degree? Because "it is God who worketh in you both to will and to work, for His good pleasure." How often you do not *will* to obey God besides the fact that you *do not* obey God. You being a truly saved person, your heart at one time had been touched. Even though you have fallen back a little, and your heart has become harder, you are still conscious within yourself of what has happened. In His mercy towards you, God's life continues to work within until one day your heart again desires to obey God. You both will to obey and are able to obey. This is none other than the life of God operating in the emotion and will of your heart. It continues to operate until you obey Him.

There was once a sister whose conscience was so much under accusation that she reckoned she would never want God's will nor would she ever again obey Him. She was in anguish to such an extent that it was as if she were merely waiting to hear the sentence of death. At that very hour, however, she had a prayer within her. She whispered to God: "O God, though I cannot desire after Your will, I beg You to give me this obedience." Strangely, the word of Philippians 2.13 supported her that day. She had now begun to understand that unless God had worked in her heart she would not have been able to pray such a prayer. Since God did work in her to pray this prayer, He most certainly caused her to will and to work for His good pleasure. He had enabled her to obey His will because such is the purpose of His working. She saw it, arose, and was full of joy.

Doing God's Previously Prepared Good Works

"We are his workmanship, created in Christ Jesus for good works, which God afore prepared that we should walk in them"

(Eph. 2.10). This work is personally accomplished by God in Christ Jesus. It may be called "God's masterpiece." What is a masterpiece? It is the best production exceeding all others. God saves people to re-create them in Christ Jesus for the very best. This is the operation of the power of life in us. This is the characteristic of the New Covenant.

Does God create us in Christ Jesus until we are satisfied with ourselves? No. He creates us in Christ Jesus "for good works." What are good works? "Works which God afore prepared that we should walk in them." Oh, how very very high is the standard. The good works which God has earlier prepared for us to do must be "good" indeed in God's eyes.

Now God will only recognize as being good what originates from "love" (Matt. 19.17): "If I bestow all my goods to feed the poor, and if I give my body to be burned, but have not love, it profiteth me nothing" (1 Cor. 13.3). Good works which issue from love are different from the ordinary kind. They are the good which flow from the life of love, the good done in love. Such can only be performed by the life of God.

Thank God for saving us, for putting His life in us that by the power of this life He is able to accomplish this masterpiece of creating us in Christ Jesus for good works which He had previously prepared for us to walk in them. This is the gospel. And this is the glory of the New Covenant.

Striving According to His Working

"His grace which was bestowed upon me was not found vain," declared the apostle Paul. How? Because he "labored more abundantly than . . . all" the other apostles. "Yet," he hastened to add, "not I, but the grace of God which was with me" (1 Cor. 15.10). He labored more abundantly not because he was healthier than others, nor because he was more diligent than the rest, but because the grace of God was with him.

Paul also wrote this: "Whom [Christ] we proclaim, admonishing every man and teaching every man in all wisdom, that we may present every man perfect in Christ." But how could he do such a work? Immediately he explains: "Whereunto I labor also, striving according to his working, which worketh in me mightily" (Col. 1.28,29). The word "mightily" may also be translated "with explosive power." In other words, what God worked in Paul was explosive power, and hence that which worked out of Paul was likewise explosive power. The apostle labored not by his soulical strength but by this divine explosive power. This power exploded within him unceasingly, causing him to strive diligently to present every man perfect in Christ. This explosive power is the operative power of the life of God. It is this power of life which enables us to labor more abundantly and strive more diligently. Such "labor more abundantly" and "striving" are evidences of the grace and the power of life within.

Hereby are we shown that God gives us grace not for the sake of making us spiritual admirers or spiritual amusers, but for the purpose of enabling us to labor more abundantly and to strive more diligently. If anyone professes himself to be a servant of the Lord and yet indulges himself in self-love—being lazy and unwilling to work—he is not only slothful but also wicked (Matt. 25.26). Such a servant is condemned by the Lord. Therefore, let us not talk vainly about doctrine: rather let us look to God and live out His grace and demonstrate His power.

Serving in Newness of the Spirit

With respect to how this life within induces us to serve lovingly and with freshness, we should note three passages of Scripture.

"Not that we are sufficient of ourselves, to account anything as from ourselves; but our sufficiency is from God; who also made us sufficient as ministers of a new covenant; not of the letter, but of the spirit: for the letter killeth, but the spirit giveth life" (2 Cor. 3.5-6).

"But now we have been discharged from the law, having died to that wherein we were held; so that we serve in newness of the spirit, and not in oldness of the letter" (Rom. 7.6).

"For he is not . . . who is one outwardly; . . . but he is . . . who is one inwardly" (Rom. 2.28,29).

By reading these three passages we can immediately recognize the great difference between the New Covenant service and the Old Covenant service. That of the Old Covenant is of the letter, while that of the New is of the spirit. The former is old, the latter is new. The one kills, the other gives life. In other words, the Old Covenant service is done according to the articles of the letter and is done as routine; whereas the New Covenant service is performed according to the spirit—that is, we move and speak and pray as the Spirit in us directs. It may therefore be concluded that the Old Covenant service is outward, while that of the New is inward. The Old Covenant service in letter results in killing life, but the New Covenant service in spirit ends up in giving life.

To put this another way, ministry in the letter is death, while ministry in the life of Christ is living. The first is old, the second is new. The one is of letter, the other is of spirit. In short, whatever is done outwardly, in oldness of the letter, is Old Covenant service; only that which is performed inwardly, in the newness of the spirit, is New Covenant service. All which comes from outside—copying or imitating—is not of that New Covenant service which is closely related to Christ and is the outcome of the inward operation of life. The New Covenant service is spiritual, apocalyptic, and fresh: for it is "of him [God], and through him, and unto him" (Rom. 11.36). The strength of service is of Him, the performance of service is through Him, and the outcome of service is unto Him. Such is serving in the spirit and in life. Such is the New Covenant service.

"Not that we are sufficient of ourselves, to account any-thing as from ourselves; but our sufficiency is from God; who also made us sufficient as ministers of a new covenant . . . (2 Cor. 3.5,6a). It is God who so works in Paul and the others as to make them sufficient to be ministers of the New Covenant.

Paul continues elsewhere by saying: "whereof I was made a minister, acording to the gift of that grace of God which was given me according to the *working of his power*" (Eph. 3.7). Paul tells us most clearly that he becomes a minister of the gospel according to the gift of the grace of God. This gift is not tongues, visions, miracles and wonders, or healing and casting out of demons (though undoubtedly Paul has all of these gifts, see 1 Cor. 14.18; Acts 13.9-10, 14.8-10, 16.9, 16-18, 18.9); neither is it excellency of speech nor of wisdom (1 Cor. 2.1). This is not a gift which suddenly comes down from heaven, but is given him by God "according to the working of his power." It is not a miraculous gift, but a gift *of grace* that is given through the working of God's power in him. Such gift enables him "to preach unto the Gentiles the unsearchable riches of Christ; and to make all men see what is the dispensation of the mystery which for ages hath been hid in God who created all things" (Eph. 3.8,9). How very great is this gift!

"CHRIST BE FORMED" AND "TRANSFORMED" AND "LIKE HIM"

As the law of life operates freely in us life will increase to the degree of having Christ formed in us (Gal. 4.19). In the measure that Christ is gradually being formed in us, in that same measure are we increasingly transformed (2 Cor. 3.18); and the goal of transformation is to be like Him (1 John 3.2). Christ formed in us is inseparable from the operation of God's life in us. To the degree that the life of God works in us to that degree is Christ being formed in us and to that degree is there the amount of our transformation. As our inside is filled with the life of Christ our outside is able to live out and manifest Christ. This is what is meant in Romans 8.29 by "to be conformed to the image of his Son." It is both Paul's pursuit and experience (Phil. 3.10, 1.20). It should be the calling as well as the practical experience of all children of God today. For us to be wholly like Him will of course have to wait until He shall manifest himself (1 John 3.2), that is to say, at the day of "the redemption of our body" (Eph. 1.14, 4.30, especially Rom. 8.23).

"Christ Be Formed"

What is meant by "Christ be formed" in us? Let us use a simple illustration. In a chicken egg there is the life of a chicken. During the first few days of hatching, if you try to fluoroscope the egg with an electric light you will not be able to discern which part is head and which part is leg. But wait until the days of hatching are nearly fulfilled and the chick within is almost ready to break open the shell. If you examine it again with an electric light you will see the complete form of a chicken within the shell. This may be termed as "the chicken being formed in the egg."

In a similar vein, then, we can say that the life of Chirst in a young Christian is not yet formed, whereas in a matured Christian it is. The life of Christ itself is perfect, though in being subject to our limitation it may not be formed in us. Paul was "again in travail" for the Galatian believers "until Christ be formed" in them (Gal. 4.19). From this we can understand how very important this matter of formation is. Paul was not using empty words here, nor was he expressing sorrow for himself. No, but he was "again in travail" for them. This requires time, love, intercession, tears, and daily expectation.

How many of God's children today have Christ formed in them? How many of those who serve the Lord are so concerned

with the spiritual condition of God's children that they are going through this kind of spiritual travail? Alas, it is here that we
need to repent, to moan, and to shed tears for our own abnormal condition and for the lack of love towards the children of
God. How the spiritual condition of some of His children is so
babyish, so abnormal, even backward. Shall the responsibility
be fully put upon them? How can we live so comfortably as if
everything is fine? Have we moaned for them and prayed for
them? Oh God, forgive us, have mercy upon us! Give us more
days to learn and to experience; give us also time to again
travail for those believers who may be similar to the Galatians.

"Transformed"

We are told by Romans 12.1-2 that in order to be
transformed we need first to present our bodies and then to
have our minds renewed. To present our bodies may be done
all at once, but transformation is a gradual process. For the
moment we shall concentrate on the relationship between the
mind (*nous*) and transformation.

"Be ye transformed by the renewing of your mind" and
"that ye be renewed in the spirit of your mind" (Rom. 12.2;
Eph. 4.23). Both these verses speak of the relation between the
renewing of the mind and transformation. The work of the
Holy Spirit always begins at the center and moves to the circumference. The spirit, being in special connection to the
mind, must first be renewed before the mind is; then shall our
conduct gradually be changed. "Repentance" is a "change of
the mind"; it is the opening of the eye. But "the renewing of
the mind" is the eye enlightened. The greater the renewal of
the mind the larger the transformation. Day by day through
the light of life God causes us to know more and to deny more
of ourselves, and also to learn more of the reality of the inner
life. Thus may we experientially put off the former manner of
the old man and put on the conduct of the new man. (We are

here dealing with the subjective side of experience. There is also the objective side of truth, concerning which a Christian has already put off the old man with its corrupt manner and has put on the new man. All these are accomplished facts in Christ. According to the original Greek, the "put away" in verse 22 of Ephesians 4 should be "having put away," and the "put on" in verse 24 should be "having put on." See also Colossians 3.9, 10). We should realize that transformation is different from regeneration in that the latter is instantaneously done while the former is a process requiring gradual and daily changes.

What is the degree of our transformation today? How is the state of our transforming condition? If we are the same now as when we first became Christians—still full of self-pity and self-love, of selfishness and self-interest, of pride and self-importance, and of doubts and cares—then it is highly questionable if we have ever met God's light. In the event we have grown colder and harder, prouder and more self-satisfied, increasingly thoughtless and independent, it must be due to sickness either in heart or in mind. We should humble ourselves and commence to deal first with our heart. We need to ask the Lord to be merciful to us, to enlighten us and give us strength to cast aside all sins and self which hinder the operation of the law of life.

The Holy Spirit has this to say: "Today if ye shall *hear his voice, harden not your hearts*" (Heb. 3.7b, 8a). May the Lord be gracious to us in causing our heart to be softened before Him. Meanwhile, we sincerely believe the word of Philippians 2.13: "it is God who worketh in you both to will and to work, for his good pleasure." For this is the characteristic and glory of the New Covenant. Praise God!

"Transformed" and "Conformed"

In Romans 8.29 and Philippians 3.10 we have the same

word "conformed." (It should be noted that this word in the original Greek is used three times in the New Testament: in Romans 8.29 and Philippians 3.21 the word is an adjective, while in Philippians 3.10 it is a verb). What is the difference between transformed and conformed? Transformed speaks of the process, whereas conformed speaks of the product. Transformed refers to the gradual development of the Lord's life in us until finally we arrive at the same form as our Lord. Conformed signifies to be so transformed as to be like the Lord. To be of the same form simply means to be poured into the same mold. A coppersmith pours the liquid copper into a mold, and thus the copper poured in takes on the form of the mold. Or take the example of cake making, in which a man puts a prepared rice dough into a mold resulting in the cake taking upon itself the form of the mold. We are to be likened to the Lord to just that extent! To the extent of being "conformed to the image of his Son" as Paul says in Romans 8.29. It means we are to be like the Lord in His glorified manhood. If man is to be really changed according to the pattern set by God, he must undergo a transformation in inner quality; that is, he must have the life of God coming into his spirit and must allow it to permeate his whole being till through the change of nature he arrives at the total transformation of image. The Spirit of the Lord works step by step; it is "from glory to glory" (2 Cor. 3.17, 18). Praise the Lord!

We would at this point return to the matter of the "heart." "But we all, with unveiled face beholding as in a mirror the glory of the Lord, are transformed into the same image from glory to glory, even as from the Lord the Spirit" (2 Cor. 3. 18). Here we have a metaphor of the mirror. We know a mirror can only reflect what faces it; that is to say, a mirror reflects the object which stands directly opposite to it. Even so, we reflect the same measure of Christ whom we see daily in our life. "With unveiled face" simply indicates that there is no veil on our face so as to be able to see Christ completely. Conversely, however, if there *is* any veil on our face then we will either fail to see Christ or will see Him only partially. Through a careful reading of 2 Corinthians 3.12-16 we come to see that the veil is produced by a heart which does not desire after the Lord.

In the former days Moses' face shone through God's speaking with him. The children of Israel were afraid of the light on Moses' face and dared not draw near to him. For this reason, whenever he went before God he took off the veil, but when he came out to the people he put it back on (Ex. 34.29-35). Here then, the veil on Moses' face betrayed the fact that the heart of the children of Israel was far away from God. And this principle has governed the children of Israel ever after: "But unto this day, whensoever Moses is read, a veil lieth upon their heart" (2 Cor. 3.15). They are afraid of the light; they do not want the light. And thus they cannot understand the Old Testament which they read.

Nevertheless verse 16 distinctly declares that "whensoever *it [the heart] shall turn to the Lord, the veil is taken away.*" Here lies the key to seeing the Lord clearly or not seeing Him clearly. If our heart is turned towards other things it will naturally be covered as by a veil. We will live as it were under a dim light and reflect only an incomplete Christ. The mirror—that is, the heart—is the problem. Consequently, whenever there seems to be a separation or veil between us and the Lord, our heart needs once again to "turn to the Lord." As the heart turns to Him we shall see clearly and our reflection will likewise be clear.

"Like Him"

We have already said that the goal of transformation is to be "like Him." To be completely like Him will come at the time of His manifestation. Then is come "the redemption of our body." In view of this, we must also mention something about the redemption of the body. In Adam's fall man's spirit dies first, then he comes under the control of the soul and becomes fleshly, and finally his body also dies (Gen. 5.5 and Rom. 8.10, 11). Death spreads from the spirit to the soul. At the time of regeneration man's spirit is made alive first, then the Holy Spirit puts to death the deeds of the body through the work of the cross (Rom. 8.13 and Col. 3.5). The Holy Spirit causes us to deny ourselves daily (Luke 9.23). By the operation of the inner life we may experience increased transformation daily both in character and in image; and thus shall we be like the Son of God. And one day He "shall be manifested, [and] we shall be like him; for we shall see him even as he is" (1 John 3.2). This is the day which Paul awaits: the day of "the redemption of our body" (Rom. 8.23). This is also reaffirmed by the word that the Lord Jesus Christ "shall fashion anew the body of our humiliation, that it may be conformed to the body of his glory, according to the working whereby he is able even to subject all things unto himself" (Phil. 3.21).

From these verses we may understand that God's salvation begins with the making alive of the spirit and ends with the redemption of the body. The "ye shall live" in Romans 8.13 refers to our living daily in the body. Scripture tells us that "resurrection" and "change" are a mystery (1 Cor. 15.51, 52). "The redemption of the body" is to have us "conformed to the body of his glory." This is indeed glorious beyond measure! The apostle John believed that this would one day be realized. Hence he proclaimed: "If he shall be manifested, we shall be *like him*; for we shall *see him* even as he is" (1 John 3.2). This is the characteristic and glory of the New Covenant! Hence let us not be dull in our faith!

"Purifieth Himself"

Although "the redemption of the body" is God's grace, the apostle John immediately follows his word "we shall be like him; for we shall see him even as he is" with: "And every one that hath this hope set on him purifieth himself, even as he is pure" (1 John 3.3). What does this hope point to? It points to the "like him" in the preceding verse. What does "purifieth" mean? There is a difference between purify and cleanse. Cleansing means to clean, that is, to have no defilement; while purification means not only being undefiled but also unmixed. How do we purify ourselves? By the light of life (John 1.4). It is through inward enlightenment that we come to know our real condition (Ps. 36.9), thus enabling us to get rid of all which displeases God. We who are made partakers of God's nature ought—according to the inward sense which the nature of God's life produces in us—to deal with sins, self, and all which is not of God's will. This is called purifying ourselves. Yet there is even a deeper purifying, about which one who has been much instructed in the Lord once wrote:

> A spiritual danger exists in those who have experienced victory and believers whose works are effective, and in whom are spiritual gifts and righteousnesses of life . . . A deeper purification comes from the revelation of God that even the things which come out of the resurrection life of Christ must not be retained. For life grows through the operation of metabolism . . . Indeed, all that really comes out of resurrection life will never pass away, because they are eternally new. Nevertheless, they must be kept in the freshness of the Holy Spirit, not just memorized in the mind. That which comes out of resurrection life will not only not pass away but will also be eternally registered in that person, being united with him and becoming part of his life. Whenever it is used in the Holy Spirit, it remains fresh and living, just as it was first seen.

We may not be able to comprehend these words at once, yet we find a ready response within us. Oh, do we have such hope towards Him? If so, we should remind ourselves of the word of the apostle John, that "every one that hath this hope set on him purifieth himself." We should rise up and walk according to the enlightening of the Holy Spirit.

GOD IS GOD IN THE LAW OF LIFE

The life of God works steadily in us towards an immense objective. "I will be to them a God, and they shall be to me a people" (Heb. 8.10c). This word reveals the heart of God. It unveils the purpose of God from eternity to eternity. God is to be our God in the law of life, and so are we to be His people in the law of life. This is a tremendous fact. Let us prove its significance through considering together various passages in the word of God.

God's Eternal Purpose

What is God after in the universe? In Genesis 2 we learn that after God had created man, He merely hinted that man should exercise his free will to choose God's life. This passage did not openly state what God desired to get in the universe. In another passage, Genesis 3, we learn that man fell into sin, but again, this passage does not uncover what the devil wished to steal away. Things remained veiled, until the day when God in proclaiming the Ten Commandments after having led the children of Israel out of Egypt to Mount Sinai, began to spell out His heart desire. Until the day our Lord Jesus was tempted in the wilderness, when that which the devil aimed at stealing was finally uncovered. Until the day that the Lord Jesus taught His disciples to pray, when He plainly unveiled the mind of God. Let us look at these unveilings more closely.

The first of the Ten Commandments is: "Thou shalt have no other gods before me." The second commandment is: "Thou shalt not make unto thee a graven image, nor any likeness of any thing that is in heaven above, or that is in the earth beneath, or that is in the water under the earth: thou shalt not bow down thyself unto them, nor serve them; for I Jehovah *thy God am a jealous God* . . ." The third commandment is: "Thou shalt not take the name of Jehovah thy God in vain . . ." And the fourth commandment is: "Remember the sabbath day, to keep it holy" (Ex. 20.3-8). These four commandments reveal the heart desire of God. They show forth the formal demand of God towards men. They spell out His purpose of redemption as well as of creation. It is none else than that *God desires to be God*. God is God, and He wants to be God among men.

There is also a great unveiling in the New Testament. It occurred when the Lord Jesus was tempted in the wilderness. It stands opposite to God's revelation on Mount Sinai. Though we are told by the books of Ezekiel and Isaiah how a cherub whom God created was judged and became the devil because of his desire to uplift himself to be equal with God and thus rebelled against Him (Ezek. 28.12-19, Is. 14.12-15), yet never had the devil come out in such openness regarding his ambition to steal God's place as is told of in the Gospels. The supreme demand of the devil in tempting the Lord was: "If thou wilt fall down and worship me." Without any consideration, our Lord reprimanded him, saying, "Get thee hence, Satan"! Our Lord also solemnly declared: "Thou shalt worship the Lord thy God, and him only shalt thou serve" (Matt. 4.9, 10). Oh! God *alone* is God!

The prayer which the Lord taught His disciples as recorded in the New Testament is also a great revelation. That prayer unveils the heart desire of God also, which is, that *God wants to be God:* "After this manner therefore pray ye: Our Father who art in heaven, hallowed be thy name" (Matt. 6.9). Only God himself can use His name in heaven, but on earth His name is used by some people in vain. God seems to hide himself as if He is non-existent. But one day our Lord instructed His disciples to pray, saying: "Our Father who art in heaven, hallowed be thy name." He instructs us to pray in this fashion so that we may declare that He is God—He alone—and none else is. We should be like the psalmist of old, proclaiming: "Glory ye in his holy name" (105.3a). We should also declare, "O Jehovah, our

Lord, how excellent is thy name in all the earth" (Ps. 8.1a). O our God, "out of the mouth of babes and sucklings thou hast perfected praise" (Matt. 21.16b).

God Wants to Dwell among Israel
to Be Their God

God is God! Yet the wonder is — He delights to dwell among men. When God commanded Moses to build Him a sanctuary He explicitly stated His reason: "that I may dwell among them" (Ex. 25.8b). Further: "I will dwell among the children of Israel, and will be their God. And they shall know that I am Jehovah their God, that brought them forth out of the land of Egypt, that I might dwell among them: I am Jehovah their God" (Ex. 29.45-46). He instructed Moses to tell the children of Israel, "I am Jehovah your God, who brought you forth out of the land of Egypt to give you the land of Canaan, and to be your God" (Lev. 25.38). Later on He further unveiled His heart desire: "I will walk among you, and will be your God, and ye shall be my people" (Lev. 26.12). God is God! This is grand! Nonetheless He comes to dwell among men to be their God!

The Word Became Flesh and Dwelt
among Men to Declare God

Now "the Word became flesh, and dwelt among us" (John 1.14a). "That which was from the beginning" — the Word of life — had become "that which we have heard, that which we have seen with our eyes, that which we beheld, and our hands handled" (1 John 1.1). "No man hath seen God at any time"; yet "the only begotten Son, who is in the bosom of the Father, he hath declared him" (John 1.18). This is "Immanuel; which is, being interpreted, God with us" (Matt. 1.23b).

God Dwells in the Church to Be God

When the church is established, being "built up a spiritual house" (1 Peter 2.5), she becomes "a habitation of God in the Spirit" (Eph. 2.22). This is indeed most mysterious and most glorious. When the Word became flesh and dwelt among men, He was nevertheless restricted by time and space; but when God in the Spirit comes to dwell in the church, neither time nor space can restrain His presence with her. Hallelujah!

God Will Be God of the House of Israel during the Kingdom Age

In spite of the fact that the children of Israel forsook God in the Old Testament time, He will establish a new covenant with them in the future. After these days, He will put His laws into their mind and write them on their heart that He may be their God (Heb. 8.10).

God Shall Dwell among Men As God in Eternity to Come

The day shall come when "the tabernacle of God is with men, and he shall dwell with them, and they shall be his peoples, and God himself shall be with them, and be their God" (Rev. 21.3). This is really too good! And God "shall wipe away every tear from their eyes; and death shall be no more; neither shall there be mourning, nor crying, nor pain, any more: the first things are passed away" (Rev. 21.4). God and men, men and God, shall never be separated! Hallelujah!

God As Father and God As God

On the day of His resurrection the Lord Jesus said to Mary Magdalene: "Go unto my brethren, and say to them, I ascend unto my Father and your Father, and my God and your God" (John 20.17b). This tells us that we have both a God and a Father. What then is the difference between God as Father and God as God? The Bible shows us that God as Father signifies His relationship with us individually, while God as God denotes His relationship with the entire universe. Speaking of Him as God points to His position — that is, He is the Lord of creation.

Knowing God as Father causes us to cast ourselves upon His bosom, whereas knowing Him as God induces us to prostrate ourselves on the ground in worship. We are God's children, living in His love and happily enjoying all that he has bestowed upon us. We are God's people, standing in our place as men worshipping and praising Him. In knowing Him as God we "worship Jehovah in holy array" (Ps. 29.2b)! Just as the psalmist sings: "In thy fear will I worship" (5.7b). If a person knows God as God, how dare he not fear Him in all things? He dare not be careless about his garments, his conduct. All who give ground to sin — being careless and loose, presumptuous and arrogant — know not God as God.

We should understand that "there is no creature that is not manifest in his sight: but all things are naked and laid open before the eyes of him with whom we have to do" (Heb. 4.13). Therefore, "have no fellowship with the unfruitful works of darkness, but rather even reprove them; for the things which are done by them in secret it is a shame even to speak of" (Eph. 5.11, 12). Whatever is done in darkness is feared to be laid open before God. They are shameful things. "Knowing therefore the fear of the Lord," says Paul, "we persuade men" (2 Cor. 5.11). How dare we not fear Him! We would persuade men that if they have really repented and are saved, they should know that "our God is a consuming fire" (Heb. 12.29). Do we misinterpret His temporary hiding as a falling asleep? Can we despise His patient endurance in waiting for us to repent? "God is not mocked" (Gal. 6.7). We must fear God.

All who know God as God will learn to be men. For in the fall we were tempted to be gods, but in deliverance we are ready to be humans. The principle of the garden of Eden is ever that by eating the fruit of the tree of the knowledge of good and evil "ye shall be as gods" (Gen. 3.5 mg.); while the principle of Calvary is to restore us to the position of man. For this reason, we will surely take the proper place of man if we know God as God.

The purpose of our Lord's birth into a carpenter's home is to be man (Matt. 13.55). His receiving the baptism of John the Baptist is likewise to be man (Matt. 3.13-16). And He thrice resisted the temptation of the devil, again in order to be man (Matt. 4.1-10). The fact that the Lord "himself hath suffered being tempted" (Heb. 2.18a) shows that He is man. Being mocked by men, He yet refused to come down from the cross because He took the place of a man (Matt. 27.42-44). If all these are true of our Lord, how much more ought we to be men!

The twenty-four elders (Rev. 4.4) are the elders of the universe (because these twenty-four have already sat down on the thrones and wear on their heads crowns of gold; moreover, the number twenty-four is not the Biblical number of the church; these must therefore be the elders of the universe — representing the angelic beings whom God created to be the elders of the universe). Knowing God as the God of creation they worship Him by declaring: "Worthy art thou, our Lord and our God, to receive the glory and the honor and the power: for thou didst create all things, and because of thy will they were, and were created" (Rev. 4.11). Until the day of the marriage feast of the Lamb, they shall still be seen to prostrate themselves and to worship God who sits on the throne (Rev. 19.4).

The angel flying in mid-heaven, having eternal good tidings to proclaim to those who dwell on the earth, says with a loud voice: "Fear God, and give him glory; . . . worship him that made the heaven and the earth and sea and fountains of water" (Rev. 14.6, 7). This is instructive of the fact that all who know God as God must worship Him. Knowing God as the Lord of creation draws out worship.

Whoever knows God as God will stand in the place of a servant and worship (Rev. 22.9). He who "sitteth in the temple of God, setting himself forth as God" must be the one who opposes the Lord (2 Thess. 2.4). And the one who performs great signs in order to deceive those who dwell on the earth into worshipping the beast must be the false Christ (Rev. 13.14, 15 and Matt. 24.23, 24). But all who know God as God will worship Him. And this will glorify Him.

God Is God in the Law of Life

Having put His laws into our mind and having written them on our heart, God will be our God in the law of life and we will be His people. The second half of Hebrews 8.10 closely follows the first half. It does not say that God will be our God on the throne; rather, it asserts that in the law of life God shall be our God and we shall be His people. The relation between us and God and God and us is in the fellowship of life. We cannot touch God if we are not living according to the law of life. Only as we live in the law of life can we be God's people and can God be our God. In order to draw near to Him—to serve and to worship Him—we must be in the law of life.

Why should God be our God in the law of life, and in the very same law we be His people? In order to explain this it will be necessary for us to go back and consider man's creation and regeneration.

We know that God is Spirit, therefore all who wish to fellowship with Him must have a spirit. In the creation of man (Adam) there is one element in him that is similar to God, and that is, he has a spirit. In Adam's fall he becomes alienated from the life of God and his spirit turns dead towards Him. But in God's redemption and at the moment man repents and believes, not only is man's spirit made alive but also he receives into him God's uncreated life. God dwells in us through the Holy Spirit; He comes into us. And thereafter we may worship Him in spirit and truth. Exceedingly plain are the words of John 4.24: "God is a Spirit: and they that worship him must worship in spirit and truth." This statement underscores the fact that worship is only possible to those who have a like element with God. Worship needs to be in the spirit; only worship in the spirit is true worship. It is not in the mind, neither in the emotion, nor in the will, but in spirit and truth: "The true worshippers shall worship the Father in spirit and truth: for such doth the Father seek to be his worshippers" (John 4.23). This is very meaningful. By connecting this verse with the succeeding verse 24, we can see that to worship God we need to know how to worship the Father. If a person has not had a father-and-son life relationship with God, he has no life in him. His spirit is dead, hence he cannot worship God. In regeneration his spirit is made alive; he becomes a child of God; consequently he is able to communicate with God. The Father seeks for such people to worship Him. Before we become His people we must first become His children. And this is why we say that in the law of life God will be our God and so will we in the same law be His people.

"Who gave himself for us, that he might redeem us from all iniquity, and purify unto himself a people for his own possession, zealous of good works" (Titus 2.14). To be God's peculiar people is to be God's own possession (Eph. 1.14). It is due to His being our God in the law of life and our being likewise His people in the same law of life that we become His peculiar people.

"He that overcometh . . . I will be his God, and he shall be

my son" (Rev. 21.7). Oh! In eternity, so far as a life relationship—that is to say, my personal relationship—is concerned,
"he shall be my son"; and so far as God's position is concerned
—that is, so far as a relationship based on our knowledge of
God goes—"I will be his God." How glorious this is!

In conclusion, let us remind ourselves of the word that
came to the apostle John: "Worship God" (Rev. 22.9c).

8 | The Characteristics of the New Covenant: (3) Inward Knowledge

We have now spoken of two essential characteristics of the New Covenant. God forgives our iniquities and remembers our sins no more. Such is the grace which He bestows on us in the New Covenant, yet this is only a process by which His eternal purpose is to be realized. No doubt, too, God will be our God and we will be His people—all according to the law of life.

Even so, the New Covenant does not end at this point. The word of God continues by stating that "they shall not teach every man his fellow-citizen, and every man his brother, saying, Know the Lord: for all shall know me, from the least to the greatest of them" (Heb. 8.11). This would signify a deeper knowledge of God, a knowing God himself. By the Holy Spirit God will bring His redeemed people to *the* spiritual peak of knowing His very own Self. Putting His laws in our mind and writing them on our heart is but God's *procedure* by which to arrive at the *deeper goal*, that of *knowing His own Self.* It is true that to fellowship with God is an end in itself, yet at the same time fellowship is also God's *means* to reach a *deeper end,* which is the *full knowledge of God.* Let us know assuredly that His purpose is to incorporate himself in us, that He may be one with us in life. Achieving this characteristic of the New Covenant depends upon the degree to which we attain this purpose of knowing God himself in the law of life.

"My people are destroyed for lack of knowledge" (Hosea 4.6a)! The lack of knowledge spoken of here is a lack of the knowledge of God. The greatest reason for Israel's apostasy and destruction lay in their not knowing the Lord. Thank God, though, that the characteristic of the New Covenant is that all who have eternal life know Him (John 17.3). Eternal life is to-day a kind of ability to know God. He will reveal His will and guide us in the law of life, enabling us to worship and serve Him and to commune with Him, so that we may grow step by step into knowing Him more and more. Let us now see how in this law of life there is no need for anyone to teach others how to know God.

THE TEACHING OF THE ANOINTING

Let us again read Hebrews 8.11: "They shall not teach every man his fellow-citizen, and every man his brother, saying, Know the Lord: for all shall know me, from the least to the greatest of them" (the "shall not" here is very emphatic in the original Greek: it may be translated "definitely not"). What is said here coincides with the word in 1 John 2.27: "As for you, the anointing which ye received of him abideth in you, and ye *need not* that any one teach you; but as *his anointing teacheth you concerning all things*, and is true, and is no lie, and even as it taught you, ye abide in him."

Why does one who has God's life need no one else to teach him? It is because the anointing of the Lord abides in him and shall teach him in all things. This is most practical. When God says "need not," it means just that! The Lord's anointing always abides in us. Sometimes His grace is so immense that we can hardly believe. Therefore God's word continues with: "and is true, and is no lie." Never let us doubt the word of God because of our own abnormal spiritual condition. What our God has said is one with what He will accomplish. We must believe His word. Then will we praise and thank Him.

What is the teaching of the Anointing? In order to understand it, we need to be reminded of three principal functions of the human spirit—intuition, communion, and conscience.*

The Spirit Has the Function of Communion

We know that as soon as we are regenerated our spirit is made alive. This is the first step towards the communion between God and man. The Holy Spirit comes to dwell within us. As God is a Spirit, He must be worshipped in spirit and truth. The Holy Spirit therefore leads us in our human spirit to worship and to fellowship with God. This speaks of the function of communion in the human spirit.

The Spirit Has the Function of Conscience

In regeneration our conscience is also resurrected. The blood of the Lord Jesus washes the conscience to make it clean and sensitive. The Holy Spirit testifies in our conscience concerning our conduct: "The Spirit himself beareth witness with our spirit" (Rom. 8.16), "my conscience bearing witness with me in the Holy Spirit" (Rom. 9.1), "I . . . being . . . present in spirit . . . have already . . . judged" (1 Cor. 5.3), "the testimony of our conscience" (2 Cor. 1.12). All of these passages speak of the function of conscience in the spirit. If we commit wrong, the Holy Spirit will reprove us in our conscience. Let us observe that whatever the conscience condemns has undoubtedly been condemned by God. Consequently, if our conscience declares a thing wrong, it must be wrong. It

---

*It is suggested that for a much more thorough analysis by the author of these three functions than is given below the reader consult Part 5 ("An Analysis of the Spirit") of Volume Two of Watchman Nee, *The Spiritual Man* (New York: Christian Fellowship Publishers, 1968), pp. 67-127. An entire chapter is devoted to each function. — *Translator*

should be repented of and confessed, and be cleansed by the precious blood of the Lord (1 John 1.9). We can serve God without fear only with a pure and clear conscience.

The Spirit Has the Function of Intuition

As the human body has its senses, so the human spirit has its sensing too. The sensing of the human spirit lies in the innermost recesses of man's being. Here are some examples from Scripture: "the spirit . . . is willing" (Matt. 26.41), "perceiving . . . that they so reasoned within themselves" (Mark 2.8), "sighed deeply" (Mark 8.12), "groaned" (John 11.33), "provoked" (Acts 17.16), "constrained by the word" (Acts 18.5), "fervent" (Acts 18.25), "purposed" (Acts 19.21), "bound" (Acts 20.22), "refreshed" (1 Cor. 16.18), and "joyed the more exceedingly" (2 Cor. 7.13). All these are the function of the spirit's intuition. (It may be said that the sensings of the spirit are as numerous as are those of the soul. This calls for the necessity of discerning what is of the spirit and what is of the soul. Only through the deep working of the cross and the Holy Spirit can we know this important distinction).

We call this sensing of the spirit "intuition," for it comes directly from the spirit. Ordinary human feelings are induced by persons, things, or events. If the cause is joyful we rejoice, if it is sorrowful we grieve. Such feelings are causal in origin, therefore they cannot be reckoned as "intuition." What we mean by intuition refers to those sensations which can be attributed to no external causes but come directly from within.

For instance, we may be contemplating doing a certain thing. It appears quite reasonable, we like it, and we decide to go ahead. Yet somehow within us is a heavy, oppressive, unspeakable sensing which seems to oppose what our mind has thought, our emotion has embraced, and our will has decided. It seems to tell us that this thing should not be done. This is the forbiddance or *restraint of intuition*.

Or take another yet opposite example. A certain thing may be unreasonable, contrary to our delight, and very much against our will. But for some unknown reason there is within us a kind of constraint, urge or encouragement for us to do it. If we do, we will feel comfortable inside. This is the *constraint of intuition*.

The Anointing Is in the Spirit's Intuition

Intuition is where the Anointing teaches us. "As for you," writes John, "the anointing which ye received of him abideth in you, and ye need not that any one teach you; but as his anointing teacheth you concerning all things, and is true, and is no lie, and even as it taught you, ye abide in him." In very clear fashion, this passage has described the way the Anointing is to teach us. The Holy Spirit dwells in our spirit, and the Anointing is in the spirit's intuition. The Anointing teaches us concerning all things. This means that the Holy Spirit will teach us in the spirit's intuition, giving our spirit a sense similar to the physical feeling experienced when the body is anointed with oil. As our spirit receives such a sensation we know at once what the Holy Spirit is speaking to us.

Just here we should be aware of the difference between "knowing" and "understanding." Knowing is in the spirit while understanding is in the mind. We come to know a thing through the spirit's intuition, and our mind is then enlightened to understand what the intuition has known. In the spirit's intuition we know the persuasion of the Holy Spirit; in the soul's mind we understand the guidance of the Holy Spirit.

The work of the Anointing is independent of any human help. It expresses its idea sovereignly. It operates in the spirit, causing the intuition of man's spirit to know its thought. Such a knowing in the spirit's intuition is called revelation in the Bible. Revelation is nothing but the unveiling by the Holy Spirit of the true character of a thing to our spirit so that we may clearly know it. This kind of knowledge is much deeper than the understanding of the mind.

Since the anointing of the Lord abides in us and teaches us concerning all things, we have no need for people to teach us. This Anointing will teach us in all things by the operation of intuition. The Holy Spirit will express His thought through the spirit's intuition because the latter has a kind of ability to know what the Holy Spirit means by His action. We therefore need only follow the dictate of intuition—and not inquire of other people nor even of ourselves—if we wish to do the will of God.*

The anointing of the Lord will teach us concerning all things. At no time will He ever fail to teach us concerning anything. Our responsibility lies in nothing else than to be taught.

A Few Stories

Let us now give some practical illustrations. Once a brother related the following story. There was a brother who used to drink heavily. He had a friend who was also a heavy drinker. It so happened that both of them became Christians. One day the younger invited the older to a meal. On the table was some wine. Seeing this, the older friend asked: "As saved people shouldn't we probably not drink?" The younger one replied, "It does not matter if we drink a little. For what we drink is 'Timothy wine.' It is permitted by the Bible." Later on they asked a preacher: "Is it all right for saved people to drink 'Timothy wine'?" "I have served the Lord for over ten years,"

---

*Yet the author acknowledges that there is a place for outward instruction as a complement to (but never a substitute for) the inward teaching, and that there is also a need to check the inner anointing against the word of God. These two points he makes clear below in the two later sections of this Chapter entitled, respectively, "Repeat Outside" and "The Scriptures Check Our Inward Sensation."—*Translator* said the preacher, "and never have I heard of this 'Timothy wine'."

A few days later, they came again to the preacher, saying, "We have stopped drinking 'Timothy wine'." "Who taught you so?" he inquired. "Nobody." "Is it the Bible that tells you so?" "No," replied the two friends, "the Bible says Timothy may have a little wine. But we do not drink because there is no permission inside us."

Do let us see that this inward forbiddance is the restraint of the law of life. For this law of life is living and powerful. It would not permit these two to drink. It speaks, it operates, and it gives sensation; and hence we must learn to respect it.

A servant of God once told this story. A brother came to him and asked whether he could do a certain thing. "Do you know in yourself?" he inquired. To which the brother immediately replied, "I know." Some days later this brother came again to ask the servant of the Lord about another matter. The latter answered him in the same way as before: "Do you know inside yourself?" "Oh, I know, I know," he again replied. The brother came back the third time, and for the third time the servant of God asked him, "What does your inside tell you?" And immediately he once more replied that he knew. At that moment God's servant said in his heart (though he did not utter anything with his lips): "Why, my friend, do you forsake the near and seek the far? You have something in you that will teach you concerning all things, and is true, and is no lie." Let me say here and now that this something is the law of life. It teaches us what we should or should not do.

The question comes down, then, to whether you and I are willing to follow this inward law. Is our heart turned to God? If our heart turns sufficiently to Him, we need not that anyone teach us because there is in us the living and the true which will surely teach us. Every child of God has had such an experience—some more, some less; all have encountered something of this nature. There is the law of life which operates within. It speaks, therefore no one else needs to speak.

We can relate still another story. There was once a Christian who loved to entertain believers. Whatever preacher he met, he would not only invite him to a meal but also give him a gift. One time he was listening to a preacher at a certain place. What the man was preaching did not seem to agree with the Bible, for he denied that Jesus Christ came in the flesh. This Christian did not feel comfortable in hearing such a sermon, but according to his usual habit he was thinking of shaking hands with the preacher and conversing with him a few moments. Yet somehow he felt something within was forbidding him to do so. After some hestitation he went home without shaking hands.

This believer was not aware of what the Scripture says about not receiving into one's house, nor giving greetings to, those self-styled preachers who confess not that Jesus Christ has come in the flesh (see 2 John 4-7). The conviction which came out from his inner life agreed perfectly with the word of the Bible. This is a knowing without the need of human help. And this is the characteristic of the New Covenant.

Why Bible Mentions "Teaching"

Perhaps some will raise the question, Are there not many places in the Bible where "teaching" is mentioned? For example: "I [Paul] sent unto you Timothy, . . . who shall put you in remembrance of my ways which are in Christ, even as I teach everywhere in every church" (1 Cor. 4.17); also: "Howbeit in the church I had rather speak five words with my understanding, that I might instruct others also" (1 Cor. 14.19). There are many other Bible passages on teaching, such as Colossians 1.28, 2.22, 3.16; 1 Timothy 2.7, 3.2, 4.11, 13, 5.17; 2 Timothy 2.2,24 and 3.16. What should we say about them? To answer this question, let us begin from our experience and then move on to the Bible.

Already Spoken Inside

The anointing of the Lord has actually taught us within, but the problem lies in our not hearing it. We should realize how very weak we are. We are feeble to such an extent that God may have spoken once, twice, five, ten or even twenty times, and yet we do not hear. Sometimes we *have* heard but we pretend to have not; we *have* understood yet we feign not having understood. Our greatest weakness before God is in the matter of "hearing": "He that hath an ear, let him hear," cautions the Lord. In each of the seven letters recorded in Revelation Chapters 2 and 3, there is this continual refrain: "He that hath an ear, let him hear." Hearing is reckoned to be most important in Scripture.

When our Lord Jesus was asked by His disciples why He used parables in addressing the multitude, He answered, "Therefore speak I to them in parables; because seeing they see not, and hearing they hear not, neither do they understand" (Matt. 13.13). In the next breath He also quoted the words from Isaiah 6.9-10: "By hearing ye shall hear, and shall in no wise understand; and seeing ye shall see, and shall in no wise perceive: for this people's heart is waxed gross, and their ears are dull of hearing, and their eyes they have closed; lest haply they should perceive with their eyes, and hear with their ears, and understand with their heart, and should turn again, and I should heal them" (vv.14-15). All these show that men deliberately do not hear the teaching and speaking within them.

Hence often it is not a matter of God not speaking from within, but is a matter of man not hearing. After God has spoken once, twice, five times, even ten times, you still do not hear. You do not hear because you are not listening. You cease hearing because you do not hear: "God speaketh once, yea twice, though man regardeth it not" (Job 33.14). Such is the condition of some of God's children today.

There is another aspect to this to be considered. All who are sick in mind, all who are highly subjective in approach, and all who are obstinate and inflexible in opinion will find it hard to "hear." Consequently, whenever our inside fails to hear God's voice or to receive the teaching of the Anointing, we should realize that something must be wrong with ourselves. The difficulty lies with us and not with the Lord.

Thank God for His long patience. He still speaks to men: "In a dream, in a vision of the night, when deep sleep falleth upon men, in slumberings upon the bed; then he openeth the ears of men, and sealeth their instruction" (Job 33.15). If you do not hear, He will even use dream and vision to teach you. Hence it is not that God does not speak; on the contrary, He has spoken too much. The trouble is that men are deficient in hearing.

Repeat Outside

In reading the epistles in the New Testament we may see how the many teachings and instructions that are there are *repetitive* in nature. They are there because of problems in the church. Often we read "Are you ignorant" or "Know ye not" (such as in Rom. 6.3,16; 1 Cor. 3.16, 5.6, 6.2,3,9,15,16,19; James 4.4). "Are you ignorant" means you have already heard and known but you deliberately ignore it and let it pass away. God says "Are you ignorant" by means of the Bible. Yet the Bible is not to be a substitute for the speaking of the inner Anointing; it merely repeats what the Anointing has already spoken in you.

Because of our abnormal spiritual state due to our neglecting the inward teaching, the Lord sends His servants to us again and again to repeat outwardly with the word of the Bible what the Anointing has already spoken in us. Since the Lord's anointing has already taught us within, why do we not learn to hear from within? Let us understand that the inward teaching and the outward instruction are complementary to each other, though the outward can never substitute for the inward. The inward words are living and full of life. Therefore, this characteristic of the New Covenant needs to be highly esteemed by each one who belongs to God.

Here we would like to briefly remind some brothers and sisters of one point. Today in helping other people, do not legislate or hand down ten commandments to them, nor instruct them with our subjective do's and don't's. We should not act like Old Testament seers, telling individuals what God's will is for each of them. For in the New Testament, there are prophets to the church but none to individuals. New Testament prophets can only point out God's will in principle; they should never try to declare God's will to each individual. This is because all of us who belong to the Lord should learn to receive the teaching of the Anointing within us. Otherwise, there would be no New Covenant. We may only confirm or repeat what God has already said or taught in men; else where would the New Covenant be? Most certainly we need to humbly receive the instructions of those who teach us in the Lord; even so, whatever we do receive must also be taught by the Anointing within us. Only thus shall we have the New Covenant. Let us ever keep in mind that "the letter killeth, but the spirit giveth life" (2 Cor. 3.6b).

Mind Renewed

The anointing of the Lord teaches us in all things in the intuition of our spirit, but sometimes our mind fails to understand the sensation in our spirit. For this reason, our mind (or *nous*) needs to be renewed, enabling us to comprehend what the Anointing is teaching us. Romans 12.2 shows us that the phrase "be ye transformed by the renewing of your mind" precedes "that ye may prove what is the good and acceptable and perfect will of God." Moreover, Colossians 1.9 indicates that to "be filled with the knowledge of [God's] will" needs to be "in all spiritual wisdom and understanding." Hence the renewing of the mind is imperative.

If our mind is not renewed we will not be able to understand the teaching of the Anointing. On the contrary, we may take *sudden* thought injected into our mind like lightning, or groundless imagination and vain reasoning, or meaningless and worthless dream or vision, as the Lord's revelation to us. All these are harmful and profitless. We acknowledge and believe that sometimes the Lord does use dreams or visions to open man's ear, as indicated in Job 33.15,16. Nevertheless, we reject those confused, meaningless, and worthless dreams or visions as being of the Lord. The renewing of the mind is therefore highly important to the understanding and comprehension of the teaching of the Anointing.

Just how, though, is the mind renewed? Titus 3.5 reads: "renewing of the Holy Spirit." Hence the work of renewing is the *work of the Holy Spirit*. Romans 12.1-2 mentions "present your bodies a living sacrifice" first and then speaks of "the renewing of your mind." Accordingly, the renewing of the mind is *based on consecration*. Ephesians 4.22,23 declares that to "be renewed in the spirit of your mind" must be preceded by experientially "put[ting] away, as concerning your former manner of life, the old man." So the renewing of the mind is accomplished *through the cross*. To be renewed in the spirit of our mind indicates that the *renewing begins in the spirit* until it reaches the mind.

As we have mentioned before, the Holy Spirit always works from the center to the circumference. If the human heart—the depth of man—is not dealt with, the renewing of the mind is impossible. And that is why the Holy Spirit first renews the spirit of the mind and then the mind itself. Putting this all together, then, we can say that as we are constrained by the love of God to present our bodies a living sacrifice, the Holy Spirit will apply the cross in us that we may experience the putting away of the old man as regards its former manner of life and in addition fill us more abundantly with the life of Christ so as to effect the renewing of the mind as well as that of the spirit. Such renewing is a constant and continuing work of the Holy Spirit. How we must pause and offer our praise and thanksgiving to God: for all are the works of His grace. We really have nothing to do except to receive His grace and praise Him.

Let us reiterate that the teaching of the Anointing in us is most real. We have not overstated the case at all in saying we need not that anyone teach us, because the law of life is operating in us. Indeed, the Bible in fact says so. Yet on the other hand we must guard against deception or any extreme, for unquestionably we need the word of the Scriptures as a check on our inward sensation.

The Scriptures Check Our Inward Sensation

Since the Holy Spirit is "the Spirit of truth" and that He is to guide us "into all the truth" (John 14.17,16.13), our inward sensation, if it is of the Holy Spirit, will undoubtedly agree with what Holy Scripture says. In case our inward sensation disagrees with the word of God, such sensation must be inaccurate. We should know that just as the inner sensation is *living*, so the outer Bible is *accurate*. The word of the Bible is accurate and certain but not necessarily living by itself. The inward sensation may be living but sometimes is neither accurate nor certain. Similarly, a train with its locomotive has steam power, yet it must have tracks. A train cannot move on tracks without a locomotive, but neither can it, with its locomotive, run without tracks It either will not run at all or will run disastrously. The Bible shows us that in coming out of Egypt the children of Israel had before them as their guide the pillar of cloud by day and the pillar of fire by night. When our spiritual condition is normal we are as though walking under blue sky and bright sun. But our spiritual condition does not always remain constant. The Bible also says that "thy word is a lamp unto my feet, and light unto my path" (Ps. 119.105). Were there no dark night there would be no need of lamp or light. When we are bright inwardly, our inner sensation is clear and sure; but when we are inwardly dark, our inner sensation tends to be confused and flickering; and so there is the need to check with the word of the Scriptures. Life plus truth becomes real and steady power. We must walk on this lasting path of both life *and* truth. Every thought and judgment of ours needs to have checked against it the word of the Bible. This will help us to walk straight ahead without turning to the left or right.

TWO KINDS OF KNOWING GOD

Let us again read Hebrews 8.11. "They shall not teach every man his fellow-citizen, and every man his brother, saying, Know the Lord: for all shall know me, from the least to the greatest of them." All who are God's people in the law of life may know Him without the need of being taught by men. This verse twice mentions the word "know"; the first instance refers to teaching every man to know the Lord, the second says that all—from the least to the greatest—shall know the Lord. In the original Greek, these two instances of "know" are given different words: the first "know" points to ordinary knowledge, whereas the second "know" means intuitive knowledge. Ordinary knowledge is objective, an external knowledge; but intuitive knowledge is subjective in nature, an inward knowledge.

We may use a parable to illustrate the difference between

ordinary knowledge and intuitive knowledge. Sugar and salt look alike. They are both white and fine. But wait until they come to your mouth, and then you know which is sugar and which is salt. For the two has each its peculiar taste. To know sugar and salt externally with the eyes is far inferior to knowing internally by tasting them with the tongue. So too is the knowledge of God. The knowledge that comes to us from outside is only ordinary knowledge; the inward knowledge is the sure one. Whenever God gives us a taste of himself inwardly we will have joy unspeakable. "Oh taste and see that Jehovah is good"! (Ps. 34.8a) Is it not strange that God my be tasted by us? It is nonetheless true: "For as touching those who were once enlightened and tasted of the heavenly gift, . . . and tasted the good word of God, and the powers of the age to come" (Heb. 6.4,5). This indicates that spiritual things may indeed be tasted. Thank God, the characteristic of the New Covenant is in letting us taste spiritual things, nay, even God himself. Oh what blessing; and how glorious it is. Hallelujah!

THREE STEPS IN KNOWING GOD

According to the Bible there are three steps in the knowledge of God. "He made known His ways unto Moses, his doings unto the children of Israel" (Ps. 103.7). "Ways" here is the same word used in Isaiah 55.9: "so are my ways higher than your ways." What the children of Israel knew were the doings of God; what Moses knew were the ways of God. Moses' knowledge of God is a step further than that of the children of Israel. Yet the intuitive knowledge of God mentioned in Hebrews 8.11 goes still further than even the knowledge of God's ways. For to know intuitively is to know the nature of God—even God himself. By putting these two passages together, we may conclude that there are three steps in our knowledge of Him. The first step is knowing God's doings; the second, is knowing His ways; and the third, knowing God himself. Knowing God's doings and God's ways are but external knowledge, whereas knowing God and His nature inwardly is a deeper and most precious experience. Let us look at them separately.

Knowing God's Doings

What is meant by knowing God's doings? His doings are the miracles and wonders which He does. The ten plagues which God sent upon Egypt and were witnessed by the children of Israel (see Exodus 7-11), the east wind which God used to divide the water and to make the sea as dry land in one night (Ex. 14.21), the living water which flowed out of the smitten rock in the wilderness (Ex. 17.6), the manna which came down from heaven daily (Ex. 16.35), and so forth—all these are God's doings. The feeding of the five thousand with five loaves and two fish till all were filled and even something was left (John 6.9-12), the blind made to see, the lame made to walk, the leper made clean, the deaf made to hear, the dead raised (Matt. 11.5), and many many other things recorded in the Gospels—these too are God's doings. Today some individuals experience their diseases healed, and travellers in danger know the protection of God. These also are His doings. But if all we know of God is His doings, we cannot be accounted as those who know Him, because such knowledge as this is both superficial and external.

Knowing God's Ways

What does knowing God's ways mean? It may be said that we know the principles by which God works. Abraham in interceding for Sodom stood on the side of God's righteousness. He knew God was a righteous God who could do nothing against His righteousness. This indicates that Abraham knew the principle of God's working. Once when Moses saw the appearing of the glory of the Lord, he immediately said to Aaron, "Take thy censer, and put fire therein from off the altar, and lay incense thereon, and carry it quickly unto the congregation, and make atonement for them: for there is wrath gone out from Jehovah; the plague is begun" (Num. 16.46). This was due to the fact that Moses knew God's principle as to how He would react to men's action. Samuel told Saul, "Behold, to obey is better than sacrifice, and to hearken than the fat of rams" (1 Sam. 15.22b). This is knowing God's way. David declared, "Neither will I offer burnt-offerings unto Jehovah my God which cost me nothing" (2 Sam. 24.24b). This too is knowing God's way.

Knowing God Himself

What is knowing God himself? Knowing His nature is knowing God himself. We have said before that each kind of life possesses its own characteristic. A fish and a bird each has its respective characteristic. The life of God too has its unique character. His nature is upright and good (Ps. 25.8, 86.5; Matt. 19.17), and holy (Acts 3.14, 2 Cor. 1.12). It will manifest itself through light. As soon as we are born again we receive the life of God, and with it God's nature. When we touch His nature in us, we touch Him. This is knowing God himself.

Suppose in the consciousness of your conscience there is a sin which must be dealt with—otherwise you will not have peace. Yet there may be within you a kind of holy sense which is even deeper than the conviction of conscience. That holy sense abhors and is repelled by sin, not for fear of its penalty, but because of hating sin itself. Such hate comes from the holy nature of God. Whenever a person touches God himself, that person's knowledge of the holiness of God is beyond human description. Sometimes, it will actually be like Job who confessed, "I had heard of thee by the hearing of the ear; but now mine eye seeth thee: wherefore I abhor myself, and repent in dust and ashes" (Job 42.5-6). Just as tiny specks of dust are made manifest under bright sunlight, so our uncleannesses are exposed under God's holiness. No wonder that when Peter met the Lord himself on that memorable day, he fell down at His knees and said: "Depart from me; for I am a sinful man, O Lord" (Luke 5.8b). Frequently, our conscience may not condemn our words and deeds, yet deep within us there is somehow a sense of uneasiness which cannot bring itself to amen them. This indicates how the sense of the nature of God's life surpasses even the feeling of the conscience. If we learn to obey, we shall touch God here. This is knowing God himself.

"Even unto this present hour we . . . toil, working with our own hands: being reviled, we bless; being persecuted, we endure; being defamed, we entreat" (1 Cor. 4.11-13a). These words of Paul written to the Corinthian believers tell us what *the nature of this life* is as well as what *the life of God can do*. When Paul touched God's nature in this manner, he touched God himself. And thus, Paul knew God.

There was once a story about two brothers who were Christians as well as being farmers. Their rice field was situated at the belt of a hill. Daily they pedaled water into their field by means of a water wheel, but daily also they discovered that the farmer at the bottom of the hill had secretly opened their dike and was stealing their water for his own field. This continued for seven or eight days. The two brothers said nothing, though they were very unhappy about it. So they went to consult a servant of the Lord who told them: "To patiently endure is not enough. Tomorrow you must first fill the field of the one who stole your water and then pedal water to your own field." The two brothers actually carried out this advice. Strangely, the more they did so the happier they became. Finally, the one who had stolen the water was so touched by their action that he came to apologize to them. From this incident we can see that due to their following the nature of God's life they were able to do such a thing and to do it quite naturally. Otherwise, they would have begrudged doing it and would have experienced regret afterwards. Only by following God's nature in them were they able to rejoice and to praise. The more they obeyed the more they knew God.

KNOWING GOD INTUITIVELY

Knowing God himself is the greatest blessing and glory of the New Covenant. God cannot be known by the flesh but in the intuition. But how are we to know God intuitively? Let us see what the Bible says.

"And this is life eternal, that they should know thee the only true God, and him whom thou didst send, even Jesus Christ" (John 17.3). This distinctly shows us that all who have eternal life know God and the Lord Jesus. In other words, whoever has eternal life comes into possession of an ability to know God intuitively, an ability which he never had before. This eternal life is the ability to know God. It is by this inner life that we come to know Him intuitively whom we have already known. Not at all like the Athenians who worshipped "an unknown God" according to the deduction of their reasonings (Acts 17.23). Should anyone profess to have eternal life and yet has never known God, his eternal life is very questionable. More precisely, such a person does not have eternal life. If we want to know God, we must first have eternal life.

"Who among men knoweth the things of a man, save the spirit of the man, which is in him? even so the things of God none knoweth, save the Spirit of God. But we received, not the spirit of the world, but the Spirit which is from God; that we might know the things that were freely given to us of God" (1 Cor. 2.11,12). This informs us that *the Holy Spirit in our spirit causes us to know the things of God.* Never can the things of God be known by what our mind comprehends, our reasoning commends, or our wisdom confirms. Consequently the Corinthian passage goes on to say: "Now the natural man receiveth not the things of the Spirit of God: for they are foolishness unto him; and he cannot know them . . ." (1 Cor. 2.14).

"That the God of our Lord Jesus Christ, the Father of glory, may give unto you a spirit of wisdom and revelation in the knowledge of him; having the eyes of your heart enlightened, that ye may know . . ." (Eph. 1.17,18). Here the apostle prayed for the regenerated Ephesian believers that they might receive the spirit of wisdom and revelation so as to really know God intuitively. Whether this spirit of wisdom and revelation is a latent power of the believer's spirit activated by God through prayer or is wisdom and revelation given to the believer's spirit by the Holy Spirit as a result of prayer, it nonetheless gives the believer "the knowledge of God." Our intuition needs wisdom and revelation.

We need wisdom to discern what is of God and what is of our own selves. We need wisdom to detect false apostles and disguised angels of light (2 Cor. 11.13,14). God-given wisdom is not given to our mind, but He gives wisdom to our spirit. He causes us to have wisdom in our intuition, and He leads us by our intuition into the way of wisdom.

We need revelation to truly know Him. The spirit of revelation is the effect of God's movement in our spirit. It enables us to sense His desire in our intuition. It helps us to perceive His move. Only thus may we come to the true knowledge of God.

God not only gives us the spirit of wisdom and revelation that we may really know Him in our intuition, He also enlightens "the eyes of our heart" for us to know. The word "heart" here is understanding (*dianoia*) in the Greek text of Stephens 1550. It is the same *dianoia* as in Ephesians 4.18 — being the faculty of knowing and understanding. Hence Ephesians 1.17-18 speaks of "know" in two ways: the first "know" is the knowing of intuition; the second, the knowing of mind. The Spirit of revelation comes to the innermost recess of the entire being. God reveals His own Self to our spirit that we may know Him intuitively. But this is only knowing Him in our intuition. Our inward man now knows, yet our outward man is still ignorant.

For this reason our spirit must enlighten our mind, causing the latter to understand the meaning in our spirit and so giving knowledge to our outward man. Revelation occurs in the spirit, but it reaches to the mind. Revelation is in the intuition of the spirit, while enlightenment falls on the mind of the soul. In the intuition we know by sensing it; in the mind we know by understanding it.

"That ye may be filled with the knowledge of his will in all spiritual wisdom and understanding, to walk worthily of the Lord unto all pleasing, bearing fruit in every good work, and increasing in the knowledge of God" (Col. 1.9-10). This passage shows us that it needs spiritual wisdom and spiritual understanding to know God's will, to do His pleasure, and to know Him in a real way.

Spiritual wisdom, as we have already seen, is given to our spirit by God. In the meanwhile, we also need to have spiritual understanding to understand the revelation which God has given to our spirit's intuition. For whereas the spirit's intuition causes us to detect the *move* of God, spiritual understanding enables us to comprehend the *meaning* of God's movement. If we seek to know in the spirit His will in all things, we will undoubtedly increase in the knowledge of God. To grow in God means to increase in our knowledge of Him. Thus shall our intuition develop greatly and our life ripen until we are filled with God.

In view of this, we ought to follow the operation of the law of life in exercising our own spirit towards a deeper knowledge of God. What we need is to know Him in a real way. May we ask Him to grant us the spirit of wisdom and revelation with spiritual understanding that we may daily increase in the true knowledge of God.

"Blessed are the pure in heart: for they shall see God" (Matt. 5.8). This verse brings us back to the matter of the heart. If the heart is pure—that is, is not "doubleminded" (James 4.8)—we shall see God. But if our heart is inclined towards things other than God, or if there is covetousness in our heart, we then will have a veil upon us and we will not be able to see Him clearly. If we therefore have opaqueness within us, the first important consideration is for us to ask God to show us whether our heart is pure or not.

"Jesus answered and said unto him, If a man love me, he will keep my word: and my Father will love him, and we will come unto him, and make our abode with him" (John 14.23). This tells us that if we love the Lord and obey Him, God will come to dwell with us, even giving us the consciousness of His presence. This word is in perfect agreement with that in 1 John 2.27: "Even as [the Anointing] taught you, ye abide in him." By following the teaching of the Anointing we keep the word of the Lord. Thus shall we abide in Him and He shall also abide in us. Such obedience comes not by compulsion but by love. Brother Lawrence once said that if our heart "can in any measure come to know God, it can do so only through love." How varied are the desires and passions of the will and heart of man. Yet, as Brother Lawrence observed, the working out of our passions "is properly love, [and] finds its sole end in God."*

We should sing the following hymn:

> *What e'er thou lovest, man,*
>   *That too become thou must;*
> *God, if thou lovest God,*
>   *Dust, if thou lovest dust.*
> *Go out, God will come in;*

---

*The Spiritual Maxims of Brother Lawrence (Westwood, N.J., Fleming H. Revell Co., 1967), pp. 21,22.—*Translator*

Die thou and let Him live;
Be not and He will be;
   Wait and He'll all things give.

CHORUS:
O, Cross of Christ, I take thee
   Into this heart of mine,
That I to my own self may die
   And rise to Thy life Divine.

To bring thee to thy God,
   Love takes the shortest route;
The way which knowledge leads,
   Is but a roundabout.
Drive out from thee the world,
   And then thy heart shall be
Filled with the love of God,
   And holy like as He.
                —FROM THE 3RD CENTURY;
                CHORUS BY A. B. SIMPSON

Oh, love is truly the most proper outlet of our passions. Love is not something forced. We love God because He first loves us (1 John 4.19). The more we love God, the closer we draw nigh to Him; the closer we are to Him, the better we know Him; and the better we know Him, the more we love Him and thirst after Him. A saint of God once said: "God gives us a heart which is so great that He alone can fill it." We may bemoan the smallness of our heart; nonetheless, all who have tasted of God will testify that the heart He has given us is a great heart indeed—a heart so big that anything less than Him can never fill it, for God alone can fill it! How much, then, does *our* heart yearn after God?

MANIFEST GOD OUTWARDLY

Our outward manifestation of God can never exceed our inward knowledge. The depth of our inward knowledge of God determines the degree of our outward manifestation of Him. In other words, outward manifestation is the result of inward knowledge. Let us view this consequence from several angles.

Manifest God in Courage and Discernment

"When it was the good pleasure of God, who separated me, even from my mother's womb, and called me through his grace, to reveal his Son in me, that I might preach him among the Gentiles; straightway I conferred not with flesh and blood: neither went I up to Jerusalem to them that were apostles before me . . ." (Gal. 1.15-17a). The courage which Paul had in preaching the gospel to the Gentiles came from his knowledge of God's Son, whom he knew through revelation. Such knowledge does not come by the flesh. He who knows the Christ in him also recognizes the Christ in other people. This is what Paul means by saying "we henceforth know no man after the flesh" (2 Cor. 5.16a). The one who knows man after the flesh will find it difficult to receive any supply of life from others because he is easily affected by the external weakness of man. Any spot in man will become the source of his criticism and will add to his pride. For this reason, whether or not a person knows the Christ in other people depends on whether he knows the Christ in himself. "Even though we have known Christ after the flesh," says Paul, "yet now we know him so no more" (2 Cor. 5.16b).

"Every spirit that confesseth not Jesus is not of God: and this is the spirit of the antichrist . . . Ye are of God, my little children, and have overcome them: because greater is he that is in you than he that is in the world" (1 John 4.3,4). Those who truly know God can also detect false apostles (2 Cor. 11.13, Rev. 2.2), false prophets (Matt. 24.11), even false brethren (2 Cor. 11.14-15). Whenever we are deceived, it must be due to our not knowing people by the Christ in us ourselves. All who really know God have the courage to declare that He who is in them is greater than he who is in the world.

Manifest God in the Fear of God

Whoever really knows God not only has the courage to testify and is not afraid of the spirit of the Antichrist, but he also possesses especially the fear of God. Paul manifested his fear of God in letting the directions of his labor be repeatedly restrained by God (Acts 16.6,7). Moreover, Paul feared God by instantly softening his attitude upon his being informed that he was reproving the high priest (Acts 23.3-5). He who really knows God is one who has the loins of his mind girded (1 Peter 1.13). He dare not be loose in his words, actions, and attitudes. Such restraint is not imposed by his own effort, but rather he is restrained or forbidden by the divine life within.

This is true in him not only when he is before others but also when he is alone. Whenever his word or deed is inconsistent with the inner life, he is immediately checked within. As soon as he touches God, he instantly becomes softened. He who is careless outwardly must first have become loose inwardly. Any Christian who is lax, who is without restraint, unchanged, and careless in word or deed is not a God-fearing person. Whoever acts one way before men and another way behind them, who behaves in one manner in the pulpit and in another manner out of the pulpit, does not fear God. To fear Him is to have the fear of God in one's heart at any time, in any place, and about any thing.

We tremble for those who profess themselves as belonging to God and yet manifest not the slightest fear of Him in their words and deeds. Hear what the Lord says to these people: "And now, my little children, abide in him; that, if he shall be manifested, we may have boldness, and not be ashamed before him at his coming" (1 John 2.28). Do we have such boldness as this in our heart when we think that one day we shall see the Lord's face? Or will we be ashamed when everything is laid bare before the Lord?

Manifest God in Worship

No one who really knows God fails to worship Him. Brother Lawrence once said that "to worship God in truth is to acknowledge Him to be what He is, and ourselves as what in very fact we are. To worship Him in truth is to acknowledge with heart-felt sincerity what God in truth is—that is to say, infinitely perfect, worthy of infinite adoration, infinitely removed from sin, and so of all the Divine attributes."* Only those who really know God are able to truly worship Him. For instance, Jacob's knowledge of God at Bethel was but external. It indeed caused him to fear; but look at his heart condition— how he bargained with God for his own profit (Gen. 28.16-22). Wait, though, till he meets the Lord at Peniel (Gen. 32.24-32). How very different was his knowledge of God by that time. A dear saint wrote a hymn (in Chinese) with sixteen stanzas to describe this very story of Jacob at Peniel. We will here freely translate only three stanzas which express Jacob's knowledge of God after that crisis.

> *In an instant, light floods my heart,*
> *   As if a torrent has broken through the dike.*
> *I see the infinite glory of God,*
> *   Which compels me to worship and to hide;*
> *Then know I the greatness of my sins,*
> *   My irregularities and my uncleannesses.*
>
> *Thou art such a God of glory.*
> *   How terrible is the Lord of Hosts;*
> *The moment I know who Thou art,*
> *   And see what Thou art,*

Ibid., p. 20. — *Translator*

I cry and I weep
I repent and I bow.

Lord, I yield, for Thou hast conquered.
  I ask for defeat because of Thy defeat,
I surrender because of my victory.
  Your weakness prostrates me,
With fear and trembling I devote my life
  To do Thy will and glorify Thy name. *

We often say, Worship God, worship God; yet how much do we actually know God himself? Have we been smitten to the ground?

Manifest God in Godliness

A person who really knows God manifests Him. And this is none other than living a godly life. Godliness is a great mystery, but since God has been manifested in the flesh (1 Tim. 3.16), this mystery has now become a revealed one. Think of it! Jesus of Nazareth is God manifested in the flesh! This glorious God-and-Man has manifested the holy and glorious life of God. And today, this life is in us and shall be manifested through us. The operation of the law of God's life in us is to meet this demand.

Let it be clearly understood that godliness is not a kind of ascetic exercise; rather, it is a kind of life consciousness, being in line with the character of God's life. For this reason the apostle Paul lists godliness among the things which a man of God should pursue: "But thou, O man of God, . . . follow after righteousness, godliness, faith, love, patience, meekness" (1 Tim. 6.11). On the day we are born again God's "divine power hath granted unto us all things that pertain unto life and godliness" (2 Peter 1.3a). And this godliness has "promise of

---

*This last stanza is written with Hosea 12.4 in view: "Yea, he had power over the angel, and prevailed; he wept, and made supplication unto him." Such a passage shows that it is only after Jacob has *apparently* triumphed over God that he is truly broken and weeps before Him. — *Translator*

the life which now is, and of that which is to come" (1 Tim. 4.8). We know that this is the promise which he [the Lord] promised us, even the life eternal" (1 John 2.25; see also Titus 1.2). When we believe in the Son of God we receive this eternal life (1 John 5.13). Through the power of the working of this life in us we may today live it out, manifesting it in our thought, word, attitude, and deed. The apostle Paul therefore declares: "We have our hope set on the living God, who is the Saviour of all men, specially of them that believe" (1 Tim. 4.10).

We already have this godly life in us, but to express the character of this life requires exercise on our part: "Exercise thyself unto godliness" (1 Tim. 4.7b). We ought to understand that whereas the fear of God is a matter of heart intention—always fearful lest in anything self is involved or that God is offended—godliness is to allow Him to be manifested in all things. To exercise oneself unto godliness means, negatively, "denying ungodliness" (Titus 2.12)—that is, denying all that is not like God—and, positively, letting God come forth in all things. Such exercise is not ascetic practice, nor is it shutting the door on everything; instead, it is *to abide in the Lord according to the teaching of the Anointing* and learn to allow the law of divine life to express the character of God's life in our daily walk (1 Tim. 2.2).

This kind of godly exercise is more profitable than physical exercise. Even though we cannot fully experience this eternal life today, we are nevertheless experiencing it day by day until one day we shall be wholly like Him. On the day when our body is finally redeemed, we shall be wholly like Him and shall fully enjoy this eternal life. This is God's eternal purpose, and this is the glory of the New Covenant. Let us praise the Lord with a heart full of hope.

We would also mention here that if we live godly in Christ we will not be able to avoid certain happenings. Said Paul to Timothy: "Persecutions, sufferings; what things befell me at Antioch, at Iconium, at Lystra; what persecutions I endured"

(2 Tim. 3.11a). Some may think that Paul could not avoid these persecutions, for he was an apostle. But just listen to what he wrote in the very next verse: "Yea, and *all* that would live godly in Christ Jesus shall suffer persecution" (v.12). It is not the apostles alone who must endure persecutions, but all who would live godly in Christ Jesus will suffer persecutions too. No one is an exception.

It is quite true that we can be Christians who go without persecution if we are a little more liberal and clever and prudent in walking somewhat according to the course of this world, if we mix more with worldly people, if we compromise some truth or count man's favor by sacrificing the truth, and if we neither seek nor obey inward sensations. Who will persecute us if we are no different from the rest of the people? Do not surmise that those Christians who suffer much persecution must have been untimely born and now live "out of luck." Rather should we view *un*persecuted Christians as those who are not living godly in Christ Jesus; for otherwise, suffering for them would be unavoidable. How correctly a believer once said: "Highly spiritual believers carry wounds, the crowns of the martyrs flash the flame of fire." However, we need not fear, for the Lord will either empower us to endure or deliver us out of our afflictions (1 Cor 10.13, 2 Cor. 1.8-10, 2 Tim 3.11b).

We would also like to observe that the exercise of godliness or living a godly life in Christ Jesus is a kind of spiritual pursuit, a kind of overflow of life. Here we will not point out those normal phenomena, but we would call attention to some sickly and deficient ones.

(1) *Laziness.* Some Christians are born lazy. They do not want to toil or to labor. They tend to use prayer or spiritual words to shield their laziness. I heard a story told by a brother: There was once a sister who had a dislike for work. She would either excuse herself as not knowing how to work or pretend that she did not have the physical strength to do the work. Later on someone arranged for her to pick a few flowers from

the garden each day for the flower vase. After a few days she quit doing it. And what was the reason she gave? It most certainly was not spiritual. We would have to say that this is a sickly phenomenon and definitely not godliness.

(2) *Rigidity*. Some Christians mistake rigidity to be godliness. They make themselves false. One brother said he met another brother who would either lower his head towards the ground or lift up his head towards heaven after a word or two. He discovered that this brother was pretending godliness. He wished to shout to him from his heart: "Brother, do not pretend!" We should know what life is: that which flows naturally. With such rigidity in a brother, neither his spirit nor his God is able to come forth. So in exercising ourselves unto godliness we always need to be living and fresh, for it is God who manifests himself through our words and attitudes.

(3) *Coldness*. When we say that all who would live godly in Christ Jesus will suffer persecutions, we mean that all who would not offend God in order to please men will incur such treatment. This does not imply that we can be unlovely or discourteous towards people. It was told that when one day a sister met another sister strolling on a hill, she greeted her and asked her where she was going. The second sister lifted up her head towards heaven and answered coldly, "I go to meet God." Do you think such self-styled godliness, such coldness, can ever draw people to God?

(4) *Passivity*. In exercising themselves unto godliness, some Christians want to learn from Madame Guyon and Brother Lawrence. This is admirable. But in learning to be like them, they tend to be passive, which is pitiable. Now in just what way will they fall into passivity? Well, such people enjoy the presence of God so much that their ears cannot hear what people say (please note that to not hear idle words is right, but not to hear important words hurts others), neither do they understand another's thoughts nor do they care for other people. Under normal conditions, how would Brother Lawrence re-

spond to a busy and noisy environment? Would it not be an inconvenience for people if they asked for a plate and he gave a spoon or if they said something once but he did not hear, or said it twice yet he did not understand? We therefore say that if the exercise of godliness falls into passivity this is abnormal.

Let us see more fully that our Lord is "the Word [that] became flesh, and dwelt among us . . ., full of grace and truth" (John 1.14). This is the great revelation of godliness. The Paul who exhorted Timothy, saying that "godliness is profitable for all things" (1 Tim. 4.8), is the Paul who also declared: "Who is weak, and I am not weak? who is caused to stumble, and I burn not?" (2 Cor. 11.29) He was that type of man who worked with his own hands (1 Cor. 4.12) and labored more abundantly than the rest of the apostles (1 Cor. 15.10). Oh, we all should honor and learn from such an example.

A Hymn of Prayer

Exercising ourselves unto godliness means letting this godly life in us be expressed so that we may live in godliness until one day we be completely like Him. There is a hymn which describes this pursuit quite well. We quote it below as our prayer.

> *O to be like Thee! blessed Redeemer;*
> *This is my constant longing and prayer;*
> *Gladly I'll forfeit all of earth's treasures,*
> *Jesus, Thy perfect likeness to wear.*

> CHORUS:
> *O to be like Thee! O to be like Thee!*
> *Blessed Redeemer, pure as Thou art;*
> *Come in Thy sweetness, come in Thy fulness;*
> *Stamp Thine own image deep on my heart.*

> *O to be like Thee! full of compassion,*
> *Loving, forgiving, tender and kind,*
> *Helping the helpless, cheering the fainting,*
> *Seeking the wand'ring sinners to find.*

O to be like Thee! lowly in spirit,
  Holy and harmless, patient and brave;
Meekly enduring cruel reproaches,
  Willing to suffer, others to save.

O to be like Thee! Lord, I am coming,
  Now to receive th' anointing divine;
All that I am and have I am bringing;
  Lord, from this moment all shall be Thine.

O to be like Thee! While I am pleading
  Pour out Thy Spirit, fill with Thy love,
Make me a temple meet for Thy dwelling,
  Fit for a life which Thou wouldst approve.
                       —THOMAS O. CHISHOLM

NEED FOR GOD'S CONTINUOUS FORGIVENESS AND CLEANSING

Our having on earth the promise of God's life—whose nature is godliness—and having the power of His life working in us to realize His eternal life, does this mean that today we are so perfect as to have no need for confession for receiving God's forgiveness and the cleansing for the precious blood? No. Let us read again Hebrews 8.12. We have already pointed out in Chapter 6 above that according to the original Greek, verse 12 of Hebrews 8 begins with the conjunction "for," which is of great significance. It shows us that "merciful to their iniquities" and "their sins . . . remember no more" is the cause; whereas the result or aim is the putting of God's laws into our mind and writing them on our heart that He may be our God in the law of life and we may be His people in the same law of life and thus possessing a deeper knowledge of Him in us. Since knowing God is the aim, it is mentioned first; forgiveness, being the means, is mentioned last. The same order is followed in Ephesians 1. "Having foreordained us unto adoption as sons through Jesus Christ unto himself" (v.5a) comes first because it refers to purpose; there then follows: "in whom [i.e., in the Beloved] we have our redemption through his blood, the forgiveness of our trespasses" (v.7a), for this speaks of process.

The very fact that before giving us life God must first forgive our sins and cleanse us tells us also how, after having God's life, undealt sin will hinder the growth of this life. In order to let God's life operate unhindered we must not allow any sin to remain in us. We need to confess to Him and obtain forgiveness; we need to confess to man and ask for his forgiveness too. Never fancy for a moment that we may exercise ourselves unto godliness to such an extent that we need never again require God's forgiveness nor the cleansing of the precious blood. On the contrary, the more a person knows God the keener is he conscious of his shortcomings and the greater is his need for the cleansing of the precious blood.

Who knows how many tears those we recognize to be saintly Christians have shed before God! For in God's light shall we see light (Ps. 36.9). In God's light we shall see our actual condition. The hidden flesh, our hidden self, will all be exposed by the light of God. Then will we truthfully say to Him: "I will declare mine iniquity; I will be sorry for my sin" (Ps. 38.18). And then we will pray: "Who can discern his errors? Clear thou me from hidden faults. Keep back thy servant also from presumptuous sins . . . Let the words of my mouth and the meditation of my heart be acceptable in thy sight, O Jehovah, my rock, and my redeemer" (Ps. 19.12–14).

Commenting on 1 John 1, a servant of the Lord once stated:

> Life creates fellowship as well as demands fellowship. Fellowship brings in light, and light calls for the blood. This is a *chain reaction*. A person who has life will undoubtedly seek for fellowship; in fellowship he will see light; seeing light he will look for the blood. These four things form a chain; they serve as cause as well as effect to one another. For life creates fellowship, and fellowship gives us more life; fellowship brings to us light, and light

deepens our fellowship; light constrains us to seek for the cleansing of the blood, and the cleansing of the blood enables us to see more light. These four things also form a *cycle:* life creates fellowship, fellowship brings in light, light gives us the cleansing of the blood. Being cleansed by the blood, we receive more life; more life means more fellowship, more fellowship brings in more light, and more light gets us more cleansing of the blood. These four things go in a cycle. This cycle makes us grow in life. A car goes forward by the turning of its wheels. The cycling of these four things is like the rotation of the wheels; each cycle carries our life forward a little more . . . It rolls on and on, thus causing us to advance unceasingly in the life of God. Whenever it ceases to move, our growth in the life of God also stops.

The above words were spoken by one who knew God as well as His word.

To sum up, then, it is highly practical for us to know God in the law of life—to know Him in our intuition. Such knowledge has no need for man's instruction. For this is the peak of the New Covenant. This is its glory. Hallelujah! Let us praise and worship Him!

Final Word

We have dwelt long on the characteristics of the New Covenant, yet for us to really know and understand it we need the revelation and enlightenment of the Holy Spirit. We must remember that "the letter killeth, but the spirit giveth life" (2 Cor. 3.6b). The Lord also says that "it is the spirit that giveth life; the flesh profiteth nothing" (John 6.63a). Apart from the Holy Spirit, nothing can make people alive.

The New Covenant is truly full of grace, riches and glory; consequently, we must ask God to give us faith. What is faith? "Now faith is assurance of things hoped for, a conviction of things not seen" (Heb. 11.1). This is a definition of faith given by the Bible. What is "assurance"? In Greek (*hupostasis*) it means "a standing under," a "support." It is that which supports what is above. Books, for example, are placed on a book shelf, and thus the book shelf supports the books. Or take a man sitting on a chair: the chair supports the man. What is the meaning of "conviction"? This word contains the idea of "proof." Thus faith is that which supports the things hoped for, so that our heart may find rest. Faith also proves in us the things not yet seen, so that we may amen from our heart what God has said. Faith is the proof of things not seen as well as the support of things hoped for.

"For how many soever be the promises of God, in him is the yea: wherefore also through him is the Amen, unto the glory of God through us" (2 Cor. 1.20). Knowing this, let us not look at our side but rather look at Him—at Christ. His blood is the foundation of the New Covenant. He has left to us as our inheritance every spiritual blessing, and He himself also is the executor of this will and testament. Can there be anything more secure than this?

God is faithful (Heb. 10.23). His faithfulness is the guarantee of His promise and covenant (Deut. 7.9, Ps. 89.33, 34). If we do not believe, we will be offending His faithfulness as though He could lie. So whenever we do not believe, we must condemn our unbelief as sin and ask the Lord to take away our evil heart of unbelief (Heb. 3.12). Let us "look unto Jesus the author and perfecter of our faith" (Heb. 12.2a). Since the Lord has created our faith (Eph. 2.8, 1 Tim. 1.14, 2 Peter 1.1), we believe He would also perfect this faith.

Oh blessed New Covenant! Oh glorious New Covenant! Let us not be slow in faith! How much we must repent and weep for our falling short of the standard set by the New Covenant! Yet oftentimes it is not because we do not seek, but because we seek in the wrong way. We seize upon the letter, we depend on ourselves. We strive and struggle till we end in sighing and pain. Now may we be delivered from this circuitous path. Let us sing the following hymn to remind ourselves.

> *Not by wrestling, but by clinging*
>   *Shall we be most blest;*
> *Wrestling only brings us sorrow;*
>   *Clinging brings us rest.*
>
> *When we stay our feeble efforts,*
>   *And from struggling cease,*
> *Unconditional surrender*
>   *Brings us God's own peace.*
>
> *Lean we all our weight on Jesus,*
>   *Who alone can save;*
> *He by might of love hath triumphed*
>   *O'er His willing slave.*

> *Yielding, we shall know true conquest;*
> *Dying, we shall live;*
> *"Not my will, but Thine" prevaileth,*
> *Victory to give.*
>
> —J. H. STUART

Finally, let us from our heart read two Scripture passages to express our hope and desire:

Now the God of peace, who brought again from the dead the great shepherd of the sheep with the blood of an eternal covenant, even our Lord Jesus, make you perfect in every good thing to do his will, working in us that which is well-pleasing in his sight, through Jesus Christ; to whom be the glory for ever and ever. Amen. (Heb. 13.20-21)

Now unto him that is able to do exceeding abundantly above all that we ask or think, according to the power that worketh in us, unto him be the glory in the church and in Christ Jesus unto all generations for ever and ever. Amen. (Eph. 3.20-21)

TITLES YOU
WILL WANT TO HAVE

By Watchman Nee

Basic Lesson Series
Volume 1 – A Living Sacrifice
Volume 2 – The Good Confession
Volume 3 – Assembling Together
Volume 4- Not I, But Christ
Volume 5 – Do All to the Glory of God
Volume 6 – Love One Another

The Church and the Work
Volume 1 – Assembly Life
Volume 2 – Rethinking the Work
Volume 3 – Church Affairs
Revive Thy Work
The Word of the Cross
The Communion of the Holy Spirit
The Finest of the Wheat – Volume 1
The Finest of the Wheat – Volume 2
Take Heed
Worship God
Interpreting Matthew
The Character of God's Workman
Gleanings in the Fields of Boaz
The Spirit of the Gospel
The life That Wins
From Glory to Glory
The Spirit of Judgment
From Faith to Faith
Back to the Cross
The Lord My Portion
Aids to "Revelation"
Grace for Grace
The Better Covenant
A Balanced Christian Life
The Mystery of Creation

The Messenger of the Cross
Full of Grace and Truth – Volume 1
Full of Grace and Truth – Volume 2
The Spirit of Wisdom and Revelation
Whom Shall I Send?
The Testimony of God
The Salvation of the Soul
The King and the Kingdom of Heaven
The Body of Christ: A Reality
Let Us Pray
God's Plan and the Overcomers
The Glory of His Life
"Come, Lord Jesus"
Practical Issues of This Life
Gospel Dialogue
God's Work
Ye Search the Scriptures
The Prayer Ministry of the Church
Christ the Sum of All Spiritual Things
Spiritual Knowledge
The Latent Power of the Soul
The Ministry of God's Word
Spiritual Reality or Obsession
The Spiritual Man
The Release of The Spirit
Spiritual Authority

By Stephen Kaung

Discipled to Christ
The Splendor of His Ways
Seeing the Lord's End in Job
The Songs of Degrees
Meditations on Fifteen Psalms

ORDER FROM:

Christian Fellowship Publishers, Inc.
11515 Allecingie Parkway
Richmond, Virginia 23235